Surviving Widowhood

Esther Goshen-Gottstein

gefen
publishing house בית הוצאה לאור גפן
JERUSALEM ◆ NEW YORK

Typesetting: Marzel A.S. – Jerusalem
Cover Design: Studio Paz, Jerusalem

1 3 5 7 9 8 6 4 2

Gefen Publishing House
POB 36004, Jerusalem 91360, Israel
972-2-538-0247 • orders@gefenpublishing.com

Gefen Books
12 New Street Hewlett, NY 11557, USA
516-295-2805 • gefenbooks@cs.com

www.israelbooks.com

Printed in Israel

Send for our free catalogue

ISBN 965-229-287-7

Library of Congress Cataloging-in-Publication Data:
Goshen-Gottstein, Esther R
[Levadi, English]
Surviving Widowhood / Esther Goshen-Gottstein
Includes bibliographical references
1. Goshen-Gottstein, Esther R. 2. Widows—Israel—Biography.
3. Goshen-Gottstein, Moshe H. (Moshe Henry), 1925- . I. Title.
HQ1058.5.I75G6813 2002 • 305.48'9654—dc21 • CIP Number: 2002075445

Contents

To my beloved sons,
daughters-in-law and grandchildren
Who enrich my life immeasurably

Introduction

"There is the solace to be derived from knowing that the grief we feel has been endured by at least one other person."

Nancy Mairs, New York Times Book Review,
February 26, 1993

Few married women will escape widowhood. As Carol Lawson pointed out in her New York Times article, dated August 30, 1990:

"There are 11.5 million widows in the United States, and projections from census data suggest that nearly 80 percent of all married women can expect to be widowed and that they will survive their husbands by about 16 years. Underlying those projections are two trends: Women live longer than men, seven years on average, and men tend to marry women younger than themselves."

This book not only helps to anticipate the limitations of life after loss but also sends a positive message: That it is possible to survive and lead a good life even after the sorrow and anguish following the loss of the person closest to one.[1]

---

1. See also Diane Cole, 1992; Tangea Tansley, 1996; Elizabeth Harper Neeld, 1997; William Wallace, 1998; Susan J. Zonnebelt-Smeenge and Robert Devries, 1999.

This message of hope is addressed primarily to widows and their families and friends who want to help them.

The book describes the inner landscape of the author, a clinical psychologist and herself a widow, as well as the scenery she faced on the outside after she lost her husband. She lays bare her feelings, doubts, fears and thoughts as she struggled to rebuild her life.

Moreover, the author addresses four aspects of widowhood, of which only the first two have been dealt with before:

1. The value of tradition and ritual in Judaism which supported her in her loss.[1]
2. The dreams she had during this period.[2]
3. The reactions of her young grandchildren to the death of their grandfather, their first experience of loss.
4. An analysis of her self-addressed talk.

The events portrayed in the book are all true, although many names and some identifying details have been changed, in order to safeguard the privacy of the people concerned.

I owe a special debt to Liza Clayton and to Beth Eilon who made many helpful suggestions after reading earlier versions of my manuscript. My grateful thanks are extended to Esther Herskovics for her careful editing of the final version of this book.

---

1. See also Maurice Lamm, 1969; Anne Brener, 1993; Anita Diamant, 1998.
2. See also Tangea Tanslea, 1996.

How Death Did Us Part

That night I mistook Moshe's death-rattle for snoring. Only when the sound grew louder, did I turn around in bed to look at him. His eyes, half closed, were rolled up. He was not breathing. Perhaps this was merely due to sleep apnea, when breathing can stop for up to two minutes. After all, Moshe did suffer from this disorder. But what if he is unconscious, I thought terror-stricken. I screamed, called out "darling" repeatedly and felt his cold, sweaty forehead. Was he alive or dead? I ran to the phone next to my bed to ask Information for the number of the ambulance service but only got a message from an answering-machine. I rushed out to the kitchen to look up the number in the phone book. When I got through to them I shouted that I urgently needed an ambulance for my husband who was unconscious, and that I had heard him make peculiar throat noises. The person on the other end asked me to reproduce the noises over the phone and inquired whether Moshe had any illness. I stammered something about his having a serious heart condition. My answer seemed to make Moshe eligible for an ambulance, since I was asked to supply his name and address and was told to wait for the ambulance which would arrive in a few minutes, outside our house, so that the driver could find the house without delay.

Grabbing my keys and coat, I hesitated for a moment whether to return to the bedroom to check on Moshe, but I lacked the courage to do so, for fear that he had died.

Before going out into the street I tried to reach our son Alon and his wife Tamara on the phone, but they slept too deeply to hear it ring; after all, it was 12.30 a.m.

As I unlocked the front door of our building, Telma and Sol, our neighbors, entered. Sensing my panic, Telma inferred that we must have been burgled. I mumbled something about Moshe being in the worst possible state and "who knows if he is still alive?" adding that I had to wait for the ambulance in the street. Sol immediately took over this assignment from me, soon to be joined by Haim, another neighbor.

"Does Alon know?" Telma asked. My negative reply spurred her on to try and call him again. With more time and patience than I had been able to muster, she finally succeeded in reaching him and he appeared within fifteen minutes. A quarter of an hour later Tamara joined him. She had first had to find one of her neighbors to sleep over, so that the children would not remain alone.

Meanwhile my nervousness grew by leaps and bounds since there was no sign of an ambulance. I seemed to have waited for hours, knowing that every minute was crucial. Later, the doctors were to tell me that the heart and brain can remain without oxygen for at most four to six minutes. Otherwise irreversible heart and brain damage ensue, probably resulting in death.

I called the ambulance station again and was assured that the ambulance would arrive at any minute. For whom does the ambulance wail? How often had I wondered when I heard the siren of a passing ambulance and uttered a silent prayer that it should not be for Moshe. But now I could only hope that it would reach him on time, flying at break-neck speed to get to him. In fact, as I went to the staircase I saw a half dozen medical orderlies and a doctor running into our building, carrying a stretcher. They asked to be directed to the patient. As soon as they saw Moshe, they jumped on his bed, lowered him unto the floor and started to perform mouth-to-mouth resuscitation.

At this point I was considered to be in the way and therefore expendable. Hence I was asked to leave the room. I could not have felt more wretched, realizing that it was touch and go whether Moshe would survive this particular health catastrophe. And there was nothing that I could do but wait patiently when, in fact, my patience was running out as fast as the sand in an egg-timer. Later that night, when I returned to our bedroom, I found the beds and floor littered with several dozen syringes and empty ampules, the debris of a campaign against death. The ampules had contained cardiac drugs which had been injected into Moshe's jugular vein, in an effort to revive him. There was also a large blood-stain on the carpet where he had lain when they had opened his jugular vein. Actually, he was no longer breathing when they arrived; nor did he have a pulse or blood pressure. In fact, he was clinically dead. The doctors and orderlies, his would-be rescuers, fought death in a desperate struggle.

In the words of Wilfred Owen, in his poem, "Asleep":

And in the happy no-time
of his sleeping
death took him by the heart.

But Moshe was resuscitated by the team which worked on him for about twenty minutes and then decided to transport him to hospital. Alon and I, and of course the doctor and driver-orderly, accompanied Moshe in the ambulance, but not before I had searched fumblingly, with knees knocking, for the envelope containing Moshe's case history. This was to enable the doctors in the emergency ward to learn the background of Moshe's present condition.

Though there was no time to lose, the Hadassah hospital on Mount Scopus, which is fifteen minutes from our home, was chosen as the most suitable one for Moshe, as their internal medicine department was on duty that night and was set up to handle his specific problems optimally. When the ambulance with Moshe arrived at the emergency ward, the good news was that Moshe was breathing with the help of a respirator. Also, he had regained his pulse and blood pressure. This meant that he was alive after having suffered cardiac arrest. (I did not know at the time that when a cardiac arrest occurs outside a hospital, only twenty to thirty percent of such patients survive.)

The bad, nay the terrible news was that Moshe was in the deepest coma and without a single reflex. I had not anticipated such a possibility which could not have shocked me more.

We were obviously back to square one: Only a little over six years ago, Moshe had remained in the deepest coma after a triple cardiac by-pass operation. It had taken three and a half months for him to reawaken, very slowly, in spite of doctors' expectations that he would remain a permanent vegetable. Had anyone ever been in two deep comas before? I wondered and waited in anguish. I felt it was almost too much for me to relive the gruesome scenario. Could this be reality or was it merely a horrible nightmare? Why was Moshe being singled out again and why was I made to suffer thus? How long was I to stand on calamity's scaffold?

Since it is almost unheard of for anyone to recover from a long, deep coma and function normally, as Moshe had done, I was sure that he was quite unique in having the double misfortune of two deep comas. Moshe had always questioned aloud "when the lightning will strike again." In fact, the certainty of its occurrence increasingly became his incubus. But each one of his doctors had reassured him that his odds for such a scenario were no greater than those of anybody else in the general population. Moshe, however, felt that he had to pack in everything now: He wanted to complete the books he was writing, to travel around the globe and see all those countries and continents to which he had not been, to take in every cultural event possible — in short: To live concentratedly. And this, in spite of severe congestive heart failure, which meant that his heart muscle was weakened and therefore could not pump his blood adequately. Moshe also had some paralysis of the left foot; his walking was altogether seriously impaired. But with him it was mind over matter — his strength of will determined his way of life, however cumbersome and strenuous it might be.

Now he was suffering from severe convulsions, opening his eyes at each convulsion. They spread throughout his body, tapering off slowly only with the help of Valium, a tranquilizer. Though the Valium would surely help to prolong his coma, we were told that convulsions would inevitably cause brain damage. Moshe also turned his head from side to side in an involuntary fashion. This was followed by small tremors. I was reminded of Parkinson's disease and shuddered at the possibility that Moshe might have acquired this dreaded condition. Standing at his bedside, I felt overcome by the guilty helplessness of the healthy in the presence of the hopelessly ill.

We were told that the first 72 hours would determine the outcome of Moshe's critical condition. Though he survived those first three days, none of his systems functioned without drugs. Moshe was not even breathing on his own: He was still on the respirator. And as if all this were not enough, he also developed a high temperature which did not react to any medication. The doctors were not certain whether this was due to the open septic wound, dating back to his cardiac surgery, or to a malfunctioning of the brain stem. They said that they would not carry out any tests on Moshe merely to satisfy their curiosity. They would do only those tests the results of which would determine differential treatment.

Yet, somehow, I had the feeling that Moshe had been fated to stay alive even now, since there is only one ambulance for cardiac emergencies in the whole of Jerusalem and it was available that night. Also there was very little traffic at night, so that the ambulance was able to get to us in the shortest possible time. In this way I shored up some hope to counter my despair. But six days into Moshe's coma the doctors were not even sure whether Moshe was brain-dead or not. That was a fact which bewildered me — it seemed to me more important than anything else to establish that issue. After all, a brain-dead person is functionally dead — only his heart is still beating. That is the reason why doctors can remove the heart for the purpose of transplantation (provided the family gives its consent) when the patient is considered to be brain-dead.

It has been said of D.W Winnicott, the British psychoanalyst (about his unfinished autobiography), "he was alive when he died." How true this was for Moshe as well, when he had his cardiac arrest.

Realizing the desperateness of Moshe's situation, Tamara phoned Jonathan, our younger son, and Yona, his wife, who were living in Toronto (where Jonathan was enrolled in a doctoral program) as soon as Moshe had been hospitalized. Alon wondered aloud whether Jonathan should not postpone his flight to Israel so that, if Moshe did reawaken once again from his coma, Jonathan could help him in his recovery. Jonathan and Yona however, were adamant that Jonathan fly home as soon as possible, in view of Moshe's critical condition. They tried to book a ticket for Jonathan on the first available plane after Rosh Hashanah, the Jewish New Year. (Moshe's cardiac arrest had occurred on the eve of Rosh Hashanah). Jonathan arrived on Thursday morning, four days into Moshe's coma. The reunion was a tearful one for both of us, and I was glad to have Jonathan at my side at this time. We all knew that he would never have forgiven himself had he not seen his father again, even though his father was unaware of his presence.

It was Rodney, our Bostonian cardiologist friend, who had lived in our apartment building six years earlier, when Moshe was so ill, who called me up when Moshe was two days into his coma — before Jonathan 's arrival in Jerusalem. Rodney had been informed about Moshe's desperate state by Tamara and now tried to convince me that Moshe was too ill to live. He told me that, with his severe cardiac congestion, Moshe had not been expected to live for more than two years after his by-pass surgery, at most four years. Yet he had survived for six more years, another miracle. Rodney felt that Moshe was worse off now than six years ago, since his heart was functioning at only twenty per cent of its normal capacity. Moreover, he was six years older and, as if all this were not enough, his circulation had deteriorated during these years. As a friend he was warning me, that if I did not want Moshe to remain a permanent vegetable, I would have to ask the doctors to stop the antibiotic treatment and cardiac medication. Worse still, I would have to request that Moshe's respirator be turned off. Rodney stressed that we could not wait too long before taking these negative measures, because Moshe's heart might be stabilized within the week, and he could then remain in a vegetative state for weeks, months and even years.

This prognosis was too dreadful to contemplate. After sobbing my heart out, I called up Tamara and Alon to share this information with them, though the time was 1 a.m. and I knew that they desperately needed their sleep. For about an hour, Alon and I weighed up the consequences of any steps we might take. For him, "God's will be done" was a paramount guideline. But I just could not get Rodney's warning, and the fearful prospects it aroused, out of my head. I finally suggested that we consult Dr. Frank, a friend and senior physician at the hospital. Alon agreed.

When we met Dr. Frank later that morning, he told us that in Israel no doctor would turn off the respirator; but there were other steps a physician might consider taking, although never active ones.

Yossi, the father of Yona, and a doctor at another Jerusalem hospital, told us a few days later that such life and death decisions were not ones that a close family member should make. I felt relieved, since I was overwhelmed by the responsibility which I could not, in good conscience, assume. How could I possibly have become actively involved in steps that would hasten the death of my own husband?

Earlier, I had asked Dr. Frank whether he had ever seen a patient who had recovered from a condition such as Moshe's. He answered quietly: "You have." Moshe's had been the one case, unique and dramatic, of a person who had reawakened from a prolonged, deep coma. In fact, as I discovered when he was awakening at the time, no such recovery had ever been medically documented before I wrote my book *Recalled to Life*, the highly unusual story of my husband who, against all hope and against all reasonable expectations, made what Oliver Sacks called "an 'impossible' recovery," regarded as miraculous by many. We, the family, had not lost faith in the possibility of his revival during those three-and-a-half months, and we supported him as he recovered from the dreadful disabilities resulting from the severe brain damage he suffered after complications during a coronary by-pass operation.

My mother, who spoke to me on the phone from London, believed that if a miracle had occurred once, it might just occur again. I was upset that she perceived me as a kind of miracle-worker and that she almost took it for granted Moshe's history could be repeated. As far as I was concerned, I did not believe that Moshe had the slightest chance of recovery. No wonder that when I went into the Intensive Care Ward where he lay, facing continuously beeping monitors, and with the hissing of his respirator in my ear, I spoke with no conviction to him when I said: "You will get better."

Alon, the inveterate optimist, could not believe that I had abandoned all hope. He reminded me that at the beginning of his previous coma Moshe also had no reflexes. As an additional infusion of hope Alon told me about the son of the head of his department who awoke from a coma after four months. I countered: "But he was eighteen years old and healthy before his trauma."

Alon fed me a further example of a comatose patient with a

positive outcome: a seventy-year-old man who had had two cardiac arrests. During the second one he was unconscious for two weeks, unable even to breathe independently. Yet he did awake from his coma.

I stubbornly clung to my hopelessness. Was it to prevent myself from becoming disappointed later? During Moshe's first coma I had collected every crumb portending hope, as Alon was doing now. But this time I felt that Moshe must be allowed to die.

Alon obtained permission to call in a neurologist friend, Dr. Derek, for a consultation, in order to determine whether Moshe's brain-stem was still functioning or whether he was brain-dead. It appears that this is not an easy fact to establish. In one of the tests Dr. Derek thought that he evinced a flicker of a reflex in Moshe's right nipple when he squeezed it. In patients not so profoundly unconscious, this test causes deep pain and can even awaken the patient from a lighter coma. I was not present at this examination, but Dr. Derek told Alon that the problem of consciousness is like a dark, unexplored continent, so that it would be impossible for anyone to make a definitive prediction about it in Moshe's case. Alon's hopes were raised somewhat after this examination, unlike my own.

Very gradually the mixture of the waters of our hopes and the cement of our doubts about Moshe's recovery hardened into the concrete of our conviction of his imminent death.

Moshe was always working against deadlines in the articles he wrote and was invariably late in getting to the publisher with them. True to form he was to be late even for his death. In fact, "life kept interrupting his dying" (as Martin Peretz, the editor of *New Republic*, wrote in his obituary for Donald Cohen in the *New Haven Diarist*, Oct. 22, 2001).

Alon and Tamara had exchanged apartments for the weekend with good friends of theirs who live near Hadassah Hospital, Mount

Scopus, so that our family could be within walking distance of Moshe. (For religious reasons we don't travel on Sabbath).

The phone rang at 6 a.m. on Saturday morning. I was told that Moshe's condition had worsened. Alon ran to the hospital while Jonathan and I followed a little more slowly. Alon managed to be present when Moshe breathed his last, only five minutes before Jonathan and I arrived. Moshe had not regained consciousness, of course. The doctor and nurse had watched the waves of his electrocardiogram cease, one by one, his life gradually fading out like Haydn's Farewell Symphony, in which the instrumentalists stop playing one after another and the symphony 'dies away.' We, the family, had been watching him die or had hoped that we were not watching him die, for six whole days.

Moshe had had an appointment with death which turned out to be as inescapable as the force of gravity. In the end, he could not defy death and his flicker of light went out.

He looked as if he were peacefully asleep. I was reminded of Shelly's words:

"Some say.... that death is slumber."

Pain had been his constant companion; at least he would never again have to suffer any pains — death had cured all his diseases. I recalled that Moshe had expressed this very idea about his mother when she died.

It occurred to me that life and death constituted a continuing process as far as Moshe was concerned, at least after his recovery from his first coma. Some parts of him had died then: First, his leadership capabilities, his ability to take initiatives, his powers of judgment, his deep interest in other people, his capacity to socialize, his spatial capabilities, and, last but not least, the state of his physical health which could deteriorate at any moment, thereby causing his death. So, slowly I had come to accept him in his last years as potentially dying, even dead. It was no longer as shocking an idea for me as it had been when he did not awaken after his coronary surgery. Moreover, Moshe had lived 'a life half dead, a living death' when he lay unconscious for over three months.

Each of us took a tearful farewell from him, Alon adding a prayer. We left Moshe's room to talk to the doctor and nurses on duty and finally watched Moshe, covered with sheet, being wheeled out of the room.

On the way home Tamara and her children met us. There were lots of tears, hugs and kisses.

We spent the rest of the day reminiscing about Moshe, crying and laughing intermittently as we recaptured a few of his thoughts and sayings, not forgetting his humor. Above all, some of the most important episodes of our joint lives passed before my mind's eye — memory has the capacity to yield its material with remarkable speed, a chain of remembrances of a lifetime triggering one another, all of them vividly present to me at that time.

I remembered how I had met him thirty-nine years previously, in 1952, shortly before Christmas, after a lecture he had given in London, on his way from Jerusalem to Oxford, on the three monotheistic religions. We had chatted for a while in the cafeteria in which a group of us had congregated after the lecture, and I had mentioned to him that I was planning to attend his workshop on Hebrew which was to take place in Newbury, one of England's delightful small towns. Yet I was surprised when, three days later, at that workshop, he actually remembered my name. Had I made that much of an impression on him? He had certainly impressed me greatly with his intellect, his humor and vivacity, as well as with his beguiling smile which, in his roundish face, bestowed on him a puckish mien. I found the combination most appealing and felt myself more and more drawn to him.

Moreover, it turned out that we shared a common cultural background, having both been born and raised in Germany for the first decade of our lives, he in Berlin and I in Leipzig. But while, several months before the outbreak of World War II, my mother, aunt, three siblings, paternal grandmother, two cousins and I moved to Engelberg in Switzerland, where we waited for my father and uncle (already in London) to obtain visas to England for all of us — a feat which they managed to achieve just in time for us to get to London three days before the beginning of the war — Moshe and his parents immigrated to what was then still called Palestine (only in 1948 was the State of Israel founded). The two sets of parents were all observant, Zionist Jews and were later to become great friends.

But Moshe and I shared far more than a common cultural background: I had studied and obtained my first B.A. in Hebrew language and literature at London University before I had switched over to studying psychology. Hence Moshe's field was not unfamiliar to me but was one that had interested me for many years. I could not have tied myself to a man whose predominant love was mathematics or engineering, or some other discipline of which I was abominably ignorant. It was vital for me to be able to understand what 'my man' was preoccupied with for most of the day.

There were also some crucial differences in our backgrounds: Moshe was an only child, while I was the oldest of four children, my youngest brother being a baby at the time of our exodus from Germany. Moreover, while both Moshe's parents were dental surgeons, my father was a businessman and my mother a full time home-maker.

It took no longer than three days for a love relationship to develop between Moshe and me. He moved to Oxford for a post-doctoral year during which he worked at the world-famous Bodleian library. But he spent much time in London to see me and to meet my family. Alternatively, I would go up to Oxford for occasional week-ends with him.

The match between him and me was considered a highly

suitable one by my family. One of my aunts expressed her delight to my mother when informed about Moshe's background and qualifications: "*Es passt so gut*" (It is so fitting), she exclaimed, "he also studied" (at a university). According to the ethos of my parent's community, boys were destined to enter their father's business, while girls, after completing high school, were meant to marry, the sooner the better. Consequently, a couple consisting of two partners, each of whom had gone to college, was considered to be quite unusual, if not to say unique — so much so that when I registered to enter University College, London, my father was convinced that I would never find a husband. "What man wants to marry a woman who is over-educated"? was his anguished *cri de coeur*. In his estimation, I would be overqualified for the job of wife, my studies clearly reducing any chance that I might ever have had of entering the holy state of matrimony. No wonder, therefore, that Moshe seemed a direct answer to my father's prayers. Is it surprising that he and all other senior family members waxed enthusiastic when Moshe appeared on the scene, prepared to rescue me from the dreaded fate of perpetual spinsterhood?

Our love for each other deepened steadily, and three months after we first met, Moshe and I decided to get married, scheduling a July wedding.

The wedding ceremony, held in a North-West London hotel, was followed by a dinner. After hearing all the speeches delivered at that dinner, Moshe absented himself for half an hour in order to write his poem of gratitude to all those who had contributed to our great day. It turned out to be a brilliant *tour de force*, composed in classic hexameters in German and English. Fortunately, a musician friend brought along the elaborate equipment used at that time to make a recording of it. The memorable first line was addressed to me:

"Lovely queen of my heart, my queen on the day of her glory."

Yudah, one of our friends who attended our wedding, never forgets to greet me with "queen of my heart" — on those rare occasions on which we meet.

We planned to separate soon after our sublime honeymoon in Italy and France. This was meant to enable me to study at the Maudsley Hospital, Institute of Psychiatry, London, for my Postgraduate Diploma in Abnormal (now we would say Clinical) Psychology, so that I would find work in Israel, in my chosen field. Moshe had to return to Jerusalem to teach at The Hebrew University after his post-doctoral year, spent in Oxford.

One of my father's close friends came to warn me against this plan, since he was convinced Moshe would not remain faithful to me during that year; after all, how could any man be trusted not to be unfaithful to his wife during such a long stretch of time?

Moshe not only returned to Jerusalem without being able to show off his new bride to whom, incidentally, he remained constant, but he also visited me twice in London during that year. In addition, he went house-hunting in Jerusalem, finally landing an apartment right in the center of the city, which had, adjoining it, what he called a "small wood." This turned out to consist of three trees next to a garbage dump, but we were supremely happy with our new home, although our cleaning lady pitied us for not even having a balcony on which to hang our laundry. We, however, could not have been more pleased.

We not only lived in this first rented apartment, but in it Moshe also worked at his desk, surrounded by his beloved books. I had meanwhile found a position in a mental health clinic, and when I became pregnant with our first son, Alon, I started to collect data for my doctorate. The topic was, most appropriately, the attitudes to first pregnancy among different cultural groups in Jerusalem. It was Moshe who persuaded me to work for a doctorate and who also helped me phrase some of the disseration, although he was a hard-to-please task-master who frequently made me erupt in tears of frustration.

It was in London that I decided to give birth to our first child. We were attending a performance of *Hamlet* at the Old Vic Theatre on the South Bank of London (the reader may be surprised to know that I cannot remember who acted Hamlet that night) when, in the interval before the final act, my waters burst. I ran to the washroom where I attempted to staunch the flow with innumerable sanitary pads from the vending-machine. Moshe and I raced by taxi to University College Hospital, situated in the West of London, with every traffic-light on the way against us. We both feared that the baby would be born in the taxi, not realizing that Alon would take another twenty hours to make his appearance, with Moshe assisting me throughout the delivery. In that era, his assistance in these circumstances was really unusual, if not to say unheard of, and was possible only at that hospital. Later, Moshe and I would joke about having missed the fifth act of Hamlet.

I pictured Moshe as a proud father of Alon, a beautiful, blue-eyed, blond haired boy. Moshe believed in the traditional division of labor, leaving the child-care entirely to me, so that he changed the baby's diaper only once in his life time, for a photographic session, donning a white apron for the occasion. But he frequently played with Alon, read to him, and was usually around for his bed-time.

When Jonathan, the brown-eyed wonder with chestnut-colored hair, arrived on the scene, almost four years later, Moshe's joy knew no bounds. He was born at the same hospital, when we were *en route* to a sabbatical in Boston. Moshe helped to "hoover" him out by the vacuum method of delivery. He worked hard for a whole day, trying thereby to spare me the labor pains.

We now had a complete family. Moshe was greatly involved in the education of both boys, who were full of curiosity, mischievous, and part and parcel of most of our activities, which included a lot of travel, to which they adapted easily.

Alon and Jonathan grew up to be warm, bright, insightful men, with a wonderful sense of humor. Both are superlative teachers in the home and with their students. Alon, thirty-five years old when Moshe's died, is the bearded brother. At the time he taught Rabbinic and Hassidic Thought at Tel Aviv University. Religion, especially prayers and meditation, are his spiritual base, which plays a large role in his life. He was married to Tamara, a good-looking, intelligent, large-hearted woman, born in California, who gave birth to their two handsome boys, Elisha, blue-eyed like his father, aged six and Neriah, brown-eyed like his mother, aged three at the time of Moshe's death. Tamara works as a birth enabler, helping to make labor a positive experience for women, who often call her the angel of delivery.

Jonathan was thirty-one when Moshe died. Like Alon, he is an observant Jew but has a more skeptical disposition than his brother. Nor does he share Alon's interest in meditation. His research is in the experimental study of memory and, unlike other members of my family, he is a fine statistician. He loves nothing so much as to tell a good joke. He married Yona, an Israeli-born warm and attractive woman, who is a lawyer with a sharp, analytic mind. She had given birth to their daughter Tal, the only one of Moshe's grand-children who inherited his cone-shaped finger-nails and his broad based nose, three years before Moshe's death. Tal's features and curly looks reminded me of Shirley Temple.

Each of my sons and their wives had six years previously helped in an inspiring way to bring Moshe back to life and to enable him to function normally again. They had put all their love, energy and ingenuity into that task, sparing no pains, though this meant an enormous expenditure of time and effort on their part. I was proud to have such children.

Another source of pride and joy, which Moshe had shared with me, was the fact that all of these adults turned out to be exceptionally caring and sensitive parents, and that each one of them played a major part in every aspect of raising their children.

But Moshe was far more than the head of his family and I could not but conjure up in my mind the image of Moshe, the great scholar, with a worldwide reputation, professor of Semitic and Biblical studies. One of his students referred to him as "the master-teacher," known for his high demands (which the good students appreciated). They came from all over the world to study with him. No wonder that he was admired at many institutions of higher learning, such as Harvard, Brandeis, New York University, Yeshiva University and the Jewish Theological Seminary, as well as the universities of Heidelberg and Frankfurt, at all of which he had taught. All this in addition to his regular appointments at the Hebrew and Bar Ilan Universities. He had published hundreds of scholarly articles and more than a dozen books and had headed several large scholarly projects.

Shlomo, a mathematician friend, teaching at Harvard, told me that Moshe was the only person he had ever met, whom he could ask any question pertaining to the Bible and its language. Though Moshe always claimed not to know the answer, he would, after some time and thought, inevitably provide a complete and exhaustive reply.

Since Moshe was highly critical and achievement-oriented, some people considered him to be rather formidable, especially when he would take off his glasses, raise one eye-brow and look quizzically at you. But his sense of humor and the ability he had to laugh at himself tempered these qualities and made him accessible to people from all walks of life.

These were some of the thoughts and images parading before my internal eye on that day, the day on which Moshe passed away.

Because it was Sabbath, we could neither call anyone nor drive anywhere until sunset, which occurred at around 6 p.m. that day. But among ourselves we made the plans for the funeral which would take place the following morning. (In Israel it is customary to bury the dead on the day on which they die — this is regarded as honoring the dead.) None of us wanted a night funeral by candle-light, after Sabbath was over. We wanted to enable as many friends, colleagues and students as possible to attend the burial, which meant we had to have announcements in the newspapers, on the radio and even on television. Of course we informed our closest relatives and friends of the news over the phone, after Sabbath.

During Sabbath we decided on whom to ask to deliver the funeral orations and in which room we would sit *shiva* (that is to say, sit on low chairs as a Jewish mourning ritual). It turned out that during the last week of Moshe's life we had each separately and silently rehearsed for this moment and had planned the funeral and *shiva* in our minds, though none of us had talked about it before now. I was reminded of one of my patients who had planned her wedding long before she could decide to marry the man whom she was dating.

I slept in the afternoon and woke up amazed, having had the following dream:

On a bus tour with Moshe, I go into another compartment in order to arrange for the next trip. When I return I see that the bus has already left. I am horrified, thinking that Moshe will be so upset and angry with me for having let him go off alone, without me. How can he manage on his own? As I chastise myself, I see a black stool with my sweater on it, in the place where the bus had parked. It is the stool on which I decided to sit during the *shiva*.

Somebody, realizing my anguish, says: "Don't worry, the
bus will come back for you too."

When I woke up I could not believe that my mind had processed the
great event of the day so speedily and so meaningfully and had
turned it into a great dream.

In the dream I react with shock to finding myself separated from
Moshe without previous warning. I worry how he will manage on
his own, in view of the fact that he was so dependent on me in daily
life, ever since he woke up from his prolonged coma. I am not yet
aware that, as of now, the pertinent question is: How will I manage
on my own in my bereavement? But the dream answers this
unasked question by comforting me with a promise of a reunion
with Moshe, albeit in an after-life: "The bus will come back for you
too."

I rushed to share the dream with my children. We were all
amazed, not only at the speed with which my mind had processed
the sad events of that morning, but also at the fact that it had
actually sent me a message of consolation.

The funeral took place the next morning at 11 a.m. and was
attended by a large crowd of people who had known Moshe.

In Jerusalem the funeral cortege assembles in a so called
funeral-parlor, which is located in the midst of a busy traffic
intersection. Here the family members of the deceased shake hands
and hug their friends. Here, a man cuts a tear into the clothing of
each of the chief mourners to signify the ripping away of a life. Here
also, the main eulogies are delivered, before the corpse, which is
wrapped in a prayer-shawl. From this assembly place the procession
wends its way by cars and buses to the cemetery, which is about
three miles away and is situated on a hill, overlooking Jerusalem.

Two of Moshe's close colleagues and friends, Moshe Greenberg,
professor of Bible, and Moshe Bar-Asher, professor of Hebrew
language, eulogized him most movingly, detailing his life's accom-

plishments. Bar-Asher, who had been one of Moshe's students, was recovering from a detached retina and had obtained special permission from his ophthalmologist to attend the funeral and to deliver a eulogy for his revered teacher. Unfortunately, however, the words of both speakers were partly drowned out by the noise of the traffic in the streets. But I heard enough to realize that they were summarizing a life full of superlative achievements. Surely, had there been a demand for a *curriculum vitae* in order to enter the world to come, these eulogies would have amply fulfilled such a requirement.

Both our sons then for the first time recited the *kaddish*, a prayer in Aramaic, said when grieving the loss of a parent or other first-degree relative.[1] Hearing it from their lips, in a choked voice, was among the most moving moments for me during the funeral. It tore me up, since the *kaddish* symbolized more dramatically than any other words, that the head of our family was no more, that Moshe had been taken from us for ever.

Alon hesitated until the moment of the actual burial as to whether he would speak at Moshe's open grave. When he did so, his words were more riveting and poignant than any others that could have been devised. How proud Moshe would have been of him that morning, had he been able to hear him! Who knows? Perhaps he could.

There was no funeral music, there were no flowers to bedeck Moshe's grave, nor did wreaths cover it. Among Orthodox Jews, it is not considered appropriate to play music or to bring flowers as a final gift to the deceased. Instead, at the completion of the funeral rites, the mourners and their friends each picked up a small stone and walked slowly with it to the grave, on which he or she deposited it. The ultimate austerity divorced from all esthetics! Could there

---

1. The mourners' *Kaddish* does not mention death or the specific person who died but, instead, praises God in generous terms.

have been a better way to symbolize the terrible reality: "From dust thou comest and to dust shalt thou return?"

Finally, the mourners walked between two lines, formed by those who had attended the funeral. True to tradition, these called out to the mourners: "May God console you, among the other mourners of Zion and Jerusalem."

I walked through the lines with my head lowered and eyes brimming with tears, unable to see who had gathered at the final leave-taking of Moshe.

We, the closest family, lingered at the grave-side after the completion of the ceremony. It is too hard, no, it is well nigh impossible to say farewell forever to the person with whom one has shared the best years of one's life. At this point, the people surrounding me seemed but shadows, without any real substance. The only thing that was real and existed was my feeling of irretrievable loss.

Mourning

"Blessed are they that mourn"
(From the opening movement
of Brahms' German Requiem)

The bottom had fallen out of my life as in an earthquake, when the ground on which one has stood firmly for years, suddenly collapses. Would I have to wait for rescue-workers to pull me out and put me back on my feet? If only I might be granted the strength to do it on my own.

First, I would have to face the traditional Jewish grief-easing mourning ritual which includes the *shiva* (literally 'seven'), that is to say, the seven days in which the next of kin (i.e., the children, parents, siblings and marriage partners) share their grief, sitting on low chairs, wearing the garments into which a tear was made at the time of the funeral and shoes fashioned without leather. All these are signs of mourning. During that week they are visited by extended family members, as well as by friends and colleagues, who try thereby not only to honor the dead but also to offer consolation to the mourners and to enable them to express their feelings of loss. When the visitors are about to leave they say to the mourners: "May God console you among the other mourners of Zion and Jerusalem."

But for Orthodox Jews, the *shiva*, unlike the Irish wake, is not an occasion at which food or drink is served (at least, not among Ashkenazi Jews), since this would be considered a distraction from the main purpose of comforting the bereaved.

Our *shiva* for Moshe lasted only three days, since according to Jewish law, *Yom Kippur* which occurred three days after the funeral, cancelled the remaining days. This meant that about three hundred people visited us during those few days, from early morning until late at night, in order to express their condolences and to enable us again and again to recount the story of Moshe's last illness, as well as to reminisce with us about him and his life. Relatives and friends came, as did colleagues and erstwhile students. It was a highly charged, emotional time for my children and me, a time to cry as I talked and listened to others talk about Moshe.

I was glad to have the opportunity during the *shiva* to meet some of those who had known Moshe at different periods of his life. In this way I obtained a more rounded picture of who he had been and what he had meant to so many different people. Above all, I was grateful that the *shiva* enabled me to express my grief uninhibitedly. To me it felt right that the days of the *shiva* should be used in this fashion. I appreciated the fact that my religion provided me with these customs and rituals to govern my behavior and legitimate my feelings at that stressful time. They seemed to me so utterly appropriate psychologically. What a relief it was not only to know *what* to do but also *how long* you have to do it. Moreover, I was thankful that my community, which behaved like an extended family, did have room for mourners, supporting me in my sorrow, especially in the initial period of grief, when it was most crucial.

I was only too aware of another positive aspect of the *shiva*: It provided an opportunity in which we, the mourners, could devote ourselves entirely to thinking about and grieving for Moshe. During those days we were absolved from fulfilling any of our usual obligations. It was a moratorium, a waiting period, set by Jewish law. None of the mourners, for instance, was permitted to prepare or to serve food — all such arrangements were handled by others. Nor were we allowed to take a bath, to wash our clothes or to have sexual relations; and the men were prohibited from shaving. In a way, our bodily needs were neglected during that period of deep mourning. Moreover, neither my sons nor I were allowed to carry out any of our usual occupations. This ruling would apply equally to a prime minister as to a cardiac surgeon. Nothing could interfere with it. This seems to me psychologically correct in so far as the mourner is, by definition, too preoccupied with his or her recently sustained loss to be able to pay full attention to anything else.

The *shiva* is a moratorium in another sense, too: Life becomes suspended at a particular moment of time, in which everything that had once been familiar is suddenly transformed into something unfamiliar. Uncertainty and disorientation take over. The mourner has to search within him- or herself to discover what his or her new identity — as mourner, or widow, or bereaved son or daughter — means.

The *shiva* is the antithesis to today's trend which, as the anthropologist Gorer pointed out, is:

> "To dispose quickly of the body and get right back to things as usual, depriving the mourner of an opportunity to grieve and to have more than token consolation from friends and family... People are often encouraged to act as if the dead person had never existed."
>
> From: *Death, Grief and Mourning*, 1985

In fact, death notices in Israeli newspapers occasionally carry the request to refrain from visits of consolation.[1]

But for the widow in Jewish, and of course in Israeli, society,

---

1. This confirms the shift from a sacred to a secular view of death (Kamerman, 1988).

there is a recourse to rituals that guide her mourning and facilitate the possibility for her to be consoled by others.[1]

The *shiva* was a time in which I personally lost the need to eat and sleep. I seemed to be disconnected from my body. It was impossible for me to absorb the presence of all of those who flooded my home, and I could not remember afterwards exactly who had and who had not been there. When it was over, I was in a state of complete and utter exhaustion. I felt that three days of *shiva* was absolutely sufficient for me.

Yona, my daughter-in-law, and her daughter Tal arrived from Toronto at the end of the *shiva*. Yona considered it inconceivable to be separated from our family at this time of grief and mourning. I personally could have imagined no better uplift than to have all my family around me — they were a real godsend. Having to take physical care of the Canadian branch of the family was a good way to prevent me from entering into a deep depression and from feeling sorry for myself. Their presence in Jerusalem meant that the closest members of my family could all be together, and could undisturbedly continue to mourn in a more personal and private way.[2]

As for myself, I was devastated, faced with the loss of the pillar on which I had leaned for more than half of my life, the person who was the main contributor to my sense of self. Without him I felt worthless and inadequate. Yet here and there I spotted glimmers of another side of myself: The one who had helped Moshe come out of his first coma and had supported him in the aftermath, the one who

---

1. When I read excerpts of my book (published in German) to German non-Jewish audiences, I was frequently told how fortunate Jews are to have the *shiva* ritual. They related how, in their country, after the funeral, the mourner has to go back to work, no time being set aside for mourning. It is 'business as usual' for them.
2. "Grief is the price we pay for love" (Queen Elizabeth II at the memorial service for British victims killed in the New York terror attacks on Sept. 11, 2001). A relationship whose loss triggers grief, Weiss (1988) calls a "relationship of attachment."

was surrounded by family and friends and was needed by her patients. So the picture was not quite as dismal as it had seemed at first. Perhaps, eventually, there could be a life for me after Moshe's death.

For many Jews who have lost contact with their tradition, reciting the *kaddish* in synagogue after the death of a parent, a twice-daily requirement in Jewish laws of mourning, is the only Jewish custom to which they still adhere.[1] After eleven months, sons stop saying *kaddish* (only in modern times, do daughters and wives who belong to Conservative or Reform congregations, also recite the *kaddish*) as a prelude to the end of the first year after the death of the parents. I feel very ambivalent about the requirement of reciting the *kaddish* at least once a day during those first eleven months after a parent's death, because it imposes a burdensome duty on the sons: It means that they have to get up very early to go to synagogue for morning prayers and/or to take time off from their work for evening prayers. I know that Moshe would not have wanted the boys to stand on their heads by making heroic efforts to get to the synagogue for either of these services. I have already told them clearly and unambiguously that when I die, they need not take this daily obligation upon themselves. Actually, knowing both Alon and Jonathan, I realize that my attempt to absolve them from this filial duty will have no effect on them. But in point of fact I would rather be remembered positively than with the thought: "I must leave everything and run off to the synagogue." As far as I am concerned, once mourning has become ritualized, as through the *kaddish*, it is apt to lose its power to heal and console.

---

1. Leon Wieseltier, in his book *Kaddish*, calls the *kaddish* his "good fortune... it saves me the task of improvising the ritual of my bereavement." (p. 39) I personally believe that there is no right or wrong way to grieve. Each person's response to loss will be different.

During the first year of mourning the children of the deceased do not go to places of entertainment such as the theater, concert or cinema; nor do they attend social functions. Marital partners, however, have no such restrictions according to Jewish law. Their grieving is confined to the heart.

Jewish mourning is limited in time: It is over, officially, after the first eleven months, when it remains only in the private domain, except on every memorial day, known as *Yahrzeit*, when a memorial candle is lit, sons again recite the *kaddish* and the family and friends visit the grave. Jewish tradition does not encourage visits to the grave except on fixed dates, such as thirty days, and then again eleven months, after the death, and on the *Yahrzeit*, which does not mean, however, that more frequent graveside visits are forbidden.

The memorial evenings, arranged by the two universities in which Moshe had taught and carried out his research, took place just over a month after Moshe's death. Both institutions consulted with us, the family, about the details of these events.

The Hebrew University memorial was held in the auditorium of the Israel Academy of Sciences and was attended by most of Moshe's colleagues in his faculty, as well as by family members and friends. In the entrance hall to the auditorium an exhibition of Moshe's books and articles had been set up by his long-term student and devoted assistant, Shraga Assif. These works were spread over two long tables, and those attending the memorial expressed amazement not only at Moshe's prolific productivity, but also at the breadth of his scholarly interests in the fields of Bible and Language. For me they concretized his prodigious learning. I felt as proud of Moshe as a mother feels of a child who has lived up to far more than his full potential.

It was important for my sons and me to have people who had known Moshe intimately over the years eulogizing him and evaluating his contributions to scholarship. Professor Zvi Werblowsky, who served as chairman of the evening, spoke about Moshe the loyal friend and evolving theologian. He dwelt not only on his generosity, as well as on his comic gift but also on his religious faith which, while it had deepened over the years, was always accompanied by absolute tolerance and lacked any shadow of zealotry.

Professor Shmaryahu Talmon, Moshe's friend and his collaborator on one of his scholarly projects, the scientific edition of the books of the Prophets, spoke eloquently of Moshe's contribution to the field of Bible studies, while Shraga gave a lively description of Moshe, his beloved and admired teacher, and the investigator of language and especially of words.[1]

The memorial evening at Bar Ilan University had a similar format, though there were different speakers, especially Professor Menahem Kadari who gave an appraisal of Moshe the Semitist, while Professor Talmon presented an academic lecture on the Qumran scrolls, dedicated to Moshe's memory.

On both occasions I shook hands with innumerable people, many of whom promised to keep in touch. It was a source of great comfort for me to be surrounded by those who experienced Moshe's death as a loss, knowing that even those who had not been his personal friends would miss him as a colleague and scholar.

All these eulogies confirmed the realization for me that not only I, but also Moshe's colleagues knew how fortunate we were to have been enriched by Moshe's presence in our midst.

I felt a sense of gratitude that both these truly dignified memorial evenings had fittingly honored the man they eulogized. How pleased Moshe would have been to witness these events and especially to listen to the eulogies! I had provided a large

---

1. I know that this eulogy cost Shraga not only many sleepless nights but also turned into a form of mourning for him and for Rachel, another of Moshe's trusted assistants. It was composed of tears.

photograph of him which was prominently displayed at these memorials, and it seemed as if Moshe was presiding, smiling at all those who had come to pay him homage.

Moshe's memorial volume appeared almost two years after his death. It was to have been a *Festschrift* on the occasion of his sixtieth birthday but another eight years were to elapse before it was published. Moshe was informed about the *Festschrift* in-the-making and knew the names of its contributors — all of them former students of his who were now professors — and the titles of their articles. To the best of his ability, he tried to hasten the appearance of this book, afraid that he might not be in a fit state to appreciate it when it would finally appear, since he might be afflicted with Alzheimer's disease, as had happened to a friend of his, under similar circumstances. It turned out that he had good reasons to be in a hurry — not due to Alzheimer's at all, even though he was unaware of the extent to which his days were numbered. However impressive his memorial volume turned out to be, I shall never cease to mourn the fact that Moshe was unable to read and enjoy this volume, put together with such love by his erstwhile students.

Throughout history, different traditions accompanied death. The manner, as well as the length of time, assumed normal for mourning, differed greatly from culture to culture. In Western culture, tradition demanded that the bereaved family mourn for a full year. This entailed wearing black and maintaining a somber attitude. As Sprang and McNeil (1995) pointed out in *The Many Faces of Bereavement* (p. 14), "The black color conveyed the message of bereavement. This badge of sorrow gave permission to the bereaved to mourn and also dictated the behavior of the observer." The mourning period was considered vital for the psychological health of the survivors. During the course of a year, with its changes of seasons and holidays, a family gradually came to accept the absence of the dead person.

Living Beyond Loss, edited by F. Walsh and M. McGoldrick (1991; pp. 176-206), exemplifies many culturally different ways of mourning to which, however, modern people are less likely to adhere than did their predecessors:

In India a widow was expected to throw herself onto the funeral pyre of her dead husband. Though this practice was outlawed by the British when they were in charge of India, it is still known to occur. But even without this practice in modern times, Indian widows still become rejects of society and therefore expendable. When their husbands die, they move from a secure social position and family to a lack of status. This is vividly portrayed in the Indian documentary film *Salvation*, which describes the life of such destitute widows, who move to an ashram where they daily sing the praises of the god — their only contribution to society — and receive a little money, food and shelter.

In Greece and Italy a widow wore black for the rest of her life after her husband's death.

In Puerto Rico, women were expected to express their sorrow dramatically through displays of seizure-like attacks and uncontrollable emotions, while in South East Asian societies men and women, in public, were expected to be composed and stoical about their feelings.

The Irish traditionally delayed a funeral for days, so that all family members could attend this event. They believed that life in this world is generally full of suffering, so that death brings a release to a better world in the afterlife. They went to great length, at wakes, to give the dead person 'a good send-off.' They were likely to get drunk, tell stories and jokes and relate to the wake as if it were a kind of party, with little or no expression of grief. Thus, Irish family members were often unable to share their pain about the loss they had sustained.

African-Americans considered it important 'to go out in style,' regardless of the cost. At a funeral, the music — spirituals sung about the pain and suffering in this world, and the joy of reuniting with the deceased relatives in the next — and the eulogies, were designed to provoke the release of emotions, as was the opening of the coffin during the funeral. Crying and the open expression of grief were encouraged. There was a lot of family and community support.

The American white Protestant culture tends to minimize all expressions and rituals for dealing with death. Funeral rituals have been taken over and commercialized by the funeral industry.

When I hear about people returning to their place of work straight after the funeral of a close relative — as was the case with President Clinton after the funeral of his mother — I cannot but feel pity for them, since they have been deprived of a time out, to bewail and bemoan their loss and even to break down with impunity. They have to put their grieving on hold. How can they be expected to put on a good front and return to 'business as usual'?

We now know that people who were not enabled to mourn properly at the time of their loss or who suppressed or avoided grief at that time — considering it unmanly or unheroic or bad for the children, or who in this way defended against depression — may have delayed mourning reactions, breaking down on a different occasion, sometimes years later. Or symptoms may emerge which are metaphoric expressions of incomplete mourning and unhealed loss. When these people are helped to achieve catharsis by expressing their sorrow, guilt and anger (for example at their fate, at the loved one who left them, or at the medical establishment which could not help), all these being appropriate reactions to loss, it is likely that the process of grief will proceed to take its normal course toward resolution, (cf. C.M. Parkes and R.S Weiss, 1983).

After his coronary by-pass and coma Moshe refused to be treated as a sick man. He regarded the very idea that he was not healthy as insulting. The only disability which he admitted to having, was his inability to walk distances. During the last weeks of his life, however, Moshe complained of bad dreams. Their message, as he told me, was that something awful would happen to him as far as his health was concerned. I made light of Moshe's fears in this respect, though this is not the way in which I relate to dreams usually. I just could not face the possibility that he might have a premonition. In fact, all along he had feared a repeat of his coma. For me it was a scenario I could not even allow myself to imagine; it was too horrible to contemplate. I felt that I no longer possessed the mental strength to help Moshe if there were a recurrence of the coma.

He had spent every free hour working on his uncompleted works. In one of his letters he explained to a friend: "I am always overworking for, having gone through these terrible months, I am always afraid of a repeat performance."

Later, I blamed myself for not having helped Moshe more speedily during his cardiac arrest: I did not immediately recognize the death rattle for what it was, never having heard it before. Consequently I did not act quickly enough to get the ambulance. I found no comfort in the thought that I was benumbed at first and needed a few minutes to act appropriately.

It was hard to admit even to myself that there was another incident which made me feel even more guilty: As we were both getting ready to retire for the night, just before Moshe had his cardiac arrest, I complained that he was coughing, and this at a time when we were about to travel to Toronto — as if it were his fault. He defended himself by simply throwing the ball back to me: "I caught the cough from you."

These turned out to be his last words.

It was I who had tried to look after him in order to prevent him from falling ill, knowing full well that any common garden variety of cold often developed into pneumonia with him, and this, in turn, was likely to cause him severe heart congestion. But Moshe did not live in an isolation ward and I was not omnipotent; he was as prone to catch any virus or bacteria as anyone else. This time it seemed that the one who was trying to prevent him from catching a cold had been the very one who infected him.

That is how I understood Moshe's last words. I believe he thought that I had clearly failed him. The idea was a terrible one for me to digest, particularly since it was the last one ever expressed by him.

There had been a situation in the past, which I now recalled, about which I also felt guilty after Moshe's death, since, at the time, I had not followed Moshe's wishes to the hilt: He had wanted us family members to learn resuscitation, in case he would ever need to be revived on account of his heart problems. On one of his sabbaticals in the United States, Moshe, Alon and I attended such classes, arranged at Harvard. However, I never really learned to do what was required in such an emergency, so that when Moshe finally became unconscious, I was not able to perform mouth-to-mouth resuscitation on him. The only way in which I allayed my guilt feelings about this was by calling to mind the fact that I could not have worked on resuscitating him and phoned for an ambulance at the same time; yet both were definitely essential in order to save his life.

It was Rodney, our cardiologist friend in Boston, who alleviated my guilt feelings.

"Nothing and no one could have saved him," he assured me. "As it was, his survival for six years after his coronary by-pass, was a miracle."

This put the picture into perspective for me — I had not been omnipotent before Moshe's cardiac arrest, and as I now realized, neither was his death due to my failing him at the end.

When, months later, I discussed the final moments of her father's life with Linda, my sister-in-law, she was full of guilt feelings about the fact that she had allowed the nurses to change his bedding when he was almost *in extremis*. Why had she not prevailed on them to leave him in peace?

It took me some time to remember that it is usual for those left behind to blame themselves for one or more incidents at the end of the life of their loved one. In a way they feel responsible for the reason of the death or the diminished quality of the last hours of the deceased. This is what had happened to me also: I was blaming myself for a host of events at the close of Moshe's life and held myself at least partially responsible for what had gone wrong.

It slowly began to dawn on me that, like millions of other women all over the world, I had been left forever by my husband. This was the way that fate had decreed. Neither Moshe nor I had any choice in this matter. Nor was there anyone who could be blamed for this state of affairs; no one had acted negligently. Moshe had inherited the tendency for heart problems from his parents; each of them had died following heart attacks and, like him before his by-pass operation, both were obese and had suffered from *diabetes mellitus*. I could be angry only at the 'bad genes' Moshe had inherited. And I could rant and rail at fate, but I soon realized that this would get me nowhere. I would just have to learn to accept what had been decreed, excruciatingly painful though it was, and to refashion myself in the process.

I felt it was just not fair, though I knew from long experience that nothing is divided fairly in this world: Neither good health nor good fortune, and least of all long life. The slices of apple pie handed out at birth, are not of equal size or even of equal quality; unhappily, many children get none at all. I had been preaching this unpalatable truth for years to my patients whenever they complained that it wasn't fair that they did not have more sensitive parents, better looks or more material means. Now I had to swallow this bitter pill myself. Nor did my previously acquired awareness of this state of affairs make the pill any sweeter. Knowing and experiencing are not identical.

Though I was able to brush off my feelings of anger at Moshe's death, many mourners strongly express their rage at what they experience as having been abandoned by their marriage partner through his or her death. Thus, Celia, a woman in her 80s, tongue-lashed Sid, her dead husband, for leaving her alone and unprotected when he died. What right did he have to predecease her, she wanted to know. Twenty-five years later, her son told me how shocked he had been at what he considered to be his mother's lack of rationality. "But dad didn't die on purpose," he had protested, "how can you be angry with him for dying?" Celia, at that stage, however, could relate to nothing but her own pain at having been left on her own, and hence the natural target on whom she vented her anger was her dead husband, Sid. Only once she had expressed her rage about what she experienced as abandonment was she able to mourn for him rather than for herself.

For as long as I knew him, Moshe felt that he was living on borrowed time, because of his predisposition to cardiac disease. He used to speak of his "untimely death," of me as his "widow" and of himself as "your late husband." I had, throughout the years, become accustomed to his morbid sense of humor, though it had at first greatly annoyed me. We were both aware throughout the years that Moshe was far from well, but I did not need to have this fact rubbed in by his constantly referring to the precariousness of his existence. While all attachments involve potential loss — the beloved could leave or even die at any time — we try not to think about this except when our noses are rubbed against this possibility.

It became impossible to ignore the message of Moshe's humor after he awakened from his coma and was left not only with residual brain damage but also with cardiac congestion. Due to my awareness of the severity of his condition, Moshe's death, though not imminent, had been a daily potentiality in my mind from that time onwards. In a way I was able to rehearse it mentally and thereby to become acquainted with it. Thus, I was preparing myself for its eventuality for six years. During that time, I also grieved inwardly for the old Moshe, the leader, the fighter, the initiator, the person who juggled half a dozen ideas at the same time, and the man with excellent social judgment. This old Moshe had died during the long coma and a 'changed' Moshe, who was more passive, more vulnerable, more dependent, but also more gentle and tolerant, took his place.

When this 'changed' Moshe also died, some of my mourning had already been accomplished. Consequently the grieving that remained was of a shorter duration than the one for those left behind by a marriage partner who dies suddenly and unexpectedly.

Beyond the rituals of the mourning process, I have observed different styles of mourning among my friends. Thus, Shula was inconsolable after she lost her husband. They had been so in tune with each other that they would finish each other's sentences. In spite of being a professional woman, Shula had greatly depended on her husband. After his death she refused to take care of even the most necessary administrative arrangements. It was as if she were thereby denying the reality which was too painful for her to face: That her beloved man was gone forever. Moreover, she refused to sleep in the bed she and her husband had shared, choosing instead to sleep on an uncomfortable couch in the living room. To top it all, although she had always been most concerned about her appearance, she no longer cared how she looked. After all, the one person whom she wanted to please was no longer there to see her.

Cynthia, who had lost her husband five years earlier, wrote to me that she was unable to get the terrible suffering of his last illness out of her head. For her, every Wednesday remained a memorial day — it was the day on which he had been hospitalized. He died on a Friday, and just as Good Friday is kept alive in the midst of Christian believers, so Cynthia turned every Friday into a day of sadness. It was as if she held on to Gerald's memory in this way and could not allow herself to let go of him. Under the circumstances, she was unable to rebuild her life and allow herself to enjoy it. She never went to see a play or film, claiming that she would not derive any pleasure from either, without Gerald at her side. Although I tried to argue with her that he would surely have wanted her to make the most of her life and to derive as much gratification from it as possible, she claimed that she was incapable of obtaining any joy by engaging in activities in which he used to share, since they would merely highlight his absence for her.

I was recently told about an inconsolable widow who declared that the only event to which she could look forward with pleasure was her own death, which would reunite her with her husband. She prevailed on an artist-friend to paint her in the arms of her late husband. The artist, after overcoming her initial objections to this unusual, if not to say grotesque assignment, painted the requested picture, whose execution troubled her deeply. Every morning thereafter, the widow set aside time to contemplate this picture. During these segments of time, she seemed transported into her happy past in which she and her husband were joined together.

I am reminded of Queen Victoria who, when Prince Albert, her husband, died, wore deep mourning for the rest of her life. She also gave orders, which were kept in force until the day of her death, that a photograph of Albert's corpse on his deathbed, surmounted by an evergreen wreath, be hung above the unoccupied side of every bed in which she would sleep. Moreover, she ordered that a clean nightshirt be placed nightly on her husband's side of the bed and a jug of hot water in his basin. Nor was anything in the prince's room allowed to be removed from the position in which it was on the night he died (E. Tisdall, 1952).

The common thread uniting these four women is that since they seemed to have sanctified the relationship with their late husbands, none of them could allow herself to let go of him. Their grief had become chronic over the years. By various means they refused to give up the former relationship, clinging to it with all their strength. The first two women did so by refusing to stop mourning their loss, while the latter two went one step further: They denied and 'undid' their husband's death. Gorer (1965) would call these "cases of mummification."

As for myself, I was determined to let Moshe go. We had had a good life together; this fact no one could take away from me. But finally I had been unable to prevent his inevitable death from overpowering him. Never was I going to forget him or to end the relationship with him in my mind. Of this I was certain. But I had an inner conviction that my life was with the living — I could not hold onto Moshe.

Widowers may, likewise, deny the death of their wives and be unable let go of them. Thus, Tony Harrison, in his poem "Long Distance," describes his father's inability to let go of his mother:

Though my mother was already two years dead
Dad kept her slippers warming by the gas
Put hot water bottles her side of the bed
And still went to renew her transport pass.

Widowers have similar problems with which to contend as do

widows. I am sure of that. But they are likely to have additional stressors:

In Western societies boys are raised in such a way as not to express their feelings as easily as do girls. One of the rules they are taught early in life is that boys do not cry. If they should do so, they are given the derogatory label of "sissy" or "cry-baby." As a result of this early education, many males consider it unmanly to cry even when one of their close family members or friends dies. They believe they have to play the role of the hero who is unaffected by even the most painful loss.

But to return to the topic of widows: Barbara, whose husband had died suddenly after a fifty-year happy marriage, commemorated him daily by going to morning prayers in synagogue for a whole year in order to recite the *kaddish* for him. This ritual form of mourning for one's husband, not uncommon among Conservative Jews, not only shaped her days but also confined her mourning to a specific period of time. Once the first year was over, she did what she could to restructure her life, helped by her personality, experience and her many friends. I admired her for it.

Five months after Moshe's death, the bank teller, a woman around forty, asked me how I was doing. She told me that she had lost her husband three years earlier, due to a sudden heart attack, leaving her behind with a two-year-old daughter. Even now she was not over his death. She was seeing a therapist to get over her depression: She just could not make her peace with such an untimely death.

I realized that a mother of small children, who has to face life alone when her husband dies, is in a particularly hard situation. Not only does she become a single parent who has to look after her children on her own, but frequently she also becomes the sole bread-winner. Thus, her inner resources become greatly depleted, especially if she has no support group like that of her own or her husband's family. However, from the moment of her husband's death, she does have a purpose in life, a reason for getting up in the morning: To look after her children, even if she is at times not in the mood to do so. Though she may feel overburdened by the tasks the children impose on her, the children provide her with activities that temporarily distract her and, when things go well, with their love and laughter, and perhaps even with a form of companionship.

How does each further death affect you? Do you become habituated, desensitized to losing yet another friend or relative, the way you become habituated to the dark? In other words, does each additional loss become less painful than the previous one? Or does every new bereavement reopen the old wound that had only recently healed, thereby increasing the pain?

Unfortunately I became a one-person experimental subject in this investigation, since fifteen months after Moshe's death, I lost three friends in the space of six weeks:

David, a friend of twenty years standing, was run over in front of his house and died in a coma three days later. The unexpectedness of his death, its purposelessness and the feeling that it could have been prevented, as well as my confrontation with yet another coma patient, caught me totally unaware and in a state of shock. I identified with David's wife, Sheila, and their children, and felt quite desolate.

A few days later Shimon, a friend whom I had met forty years earlier on the ship that brought us both on a visit to Israel, died of cardiac arrest. I was too numb from David's loss to respond with anguish.

When Anni, my longest-standing friend, died of breast cancer a month thereafter, it took me a day or two to absorb the news. I felt less involved emotionally, at first, though Anni had practically raised me between the ages of eight and ten years when she came to live with us in Leipzig, prior to our emigration. In spite of her being eleven years older than I, we became very close friends; in fact, she was more like a beloved family member. She lived in Tel Aviv, but we were in regular phone contact once I came to Israel. I shared much of my life with her, especially the traumatic times of Moshe's long coma and the aftermath of his death. Besides being physically beautiful, she was the warmest, most nurturing person I have ever encountered — every one of her meals was a feast for the eyes as well as for the taste-buds — with an openness to hear the other person and the wisdom of long experience. I can say without exaggeration: She was an ideal mother-figure, besides being a wonderful friend.

As with Moshe, I had enough time to prepare myself for Anni's loss, because we all knew about the severity of her illness. She started getting chemotherapy fifteen months prior to her death and continued to live as normal a life as possible, running her household almost unaided. But seeing her great suffering and total helplessness during the last week of her life made me wish and pray for her speedy release from such misery.

At her funeral everyone around me was crying; I was surprised that this did not affect me and that I did not shed more than a few tears. Had I become so desensitized to loss, even when it concerned someone so close to me as Anni, and when the reality of her death stared me in the eyes as they lowered her body into the grave? (In Israel, people are not buried in coffins but merely in a shroud). At the end of the burial ceremony, Anni's relatives and friends, who were not Orthodox Jews, heaped bouquets of flowers onto her fresh grave, creating a riot of diverse colors and shapes, almost too beautiful to behold. Anni had, at an earlier stage of her life, worked in a flower shop and had always been surrounded by flowers. Her grave, totally decked out with these gorgeous blooms, symbolized for me, more than the actual lowering of her body into the grave had done, that Anni was gone forever. At that point I burst into uncontrollable sobbing, which I felt would never end, coming as it did, from my very depth.

Faced with biological death, we inevitably think of immortality which according to Robert Jay Lifton (1967, p. 22), "represents a compelling, universal urge to maintain an inner sense of continuity over time and space, with the various elements of life."

Lifton describes three modes of immortality:

A. The biological mode
   "The sense of living on through, with, or even in one's sons and daughters, by imagining an endless chain of biological attachments."
B. The theological mode, expressed by various religions, concerning a life after death.
C. The mode that is achieved through a man's works, writings, art, inventions or the lasting influence of any kind that he exerts on other human beings. Thus, scholars, artists, scientists "can all share in a sense of being outlived by what they have done or created."

These different modes of immortality are all relevant for Moshe. Strange as it may sound, I am not certain whether Moshe believed in a life after death, since he never talked about it to me. My feeling is that his fears of physical suffering on earth were not balanced by a belief in an afterlife without such suffering, or in one of salvation. Nor did he ever mention a reunion after death. I suspect that he was too rational to hold such beliefs, unless he feared to talk about his own death in such direct terms, lest it should thereby become operative. What Moshe was concerned about and frequently discussed with me was his children's future, including their careers, and his unfinished projects.

Moshe certainly had a continuing family: His children carry his genes and his name, and he was able to pass his tradition and values on to the next generation. Moreover, through his teaching and scholarly writings, he achieved a lasting influence on his students and on other human beings. His writings certainly outlive him. So, in a very real sense, I know that Moshe has transcended death.

Living with Loss

Once the *shiva* was over I was determined not to allow my children to put their normal lives on hold. Therefore I wanted Jonathan and his family to return to Toronto at the end of the Jewish festivals, so that the he could complete his doctoral program. After they left, I felt an emptiness around me, an absence, a desolation.

But from the start of Moshe's final illness, I tried not to play hide-and-seek with my reality, however stressful it might be, which is why I returned to Moshe's-and-my bedroom after having helped to hospitalize him. Tamara had suggested that I sleep in a different room that night and wait until someone else clean up our bedroom in the morning. However, I preferred to sleep in my own bed. The empty ampules, with whose content the medics had tried to revive Moshe, were strewn all over the bed and floor, and there was a large blood-stain on the carpet, the result of their attempt to resuscitate him. I gritted my teeth, picked up the empty ampules and retired for the night. The events of the past few hours raced through my head wildly and would not leave me for a long time. But finally I fell into a sleep of utter exhaustion.

Daily life had to continue. At first, when Moshe was hospitalized, Nehama, one of Yona's sisters, insisted on moving in with me. She said I would not see or feel her in the apartment, unless I wanted to do so. Clearly she is a person with much tact, whom I like and respect greatly. I gratefully accepted her offer and felt good that I had the possibility of talking to her in the evenings and at meal times.

Jonathan and Yona suggested that I go with them to Toronto, at least for a while, in order to prevent my having to be on my own. It required no special deliberation on my part to turn down their generous offer. Intuitively I realized that I needed to stay at home and to start making a new life for myself in my own apartment, in my home-town, where I felt most at ease. I saw no sense in deferring the swallowing of the bitter pill; sooner or later I would have to face the reality that I was alone now. So why postpone the misery?

Moreover, I did not have only Alon and Tamara, as well as their little boys, living near me in Jerusalem, but also numerous friends whom I would not have had in Toronto.

A point of major importance in my firm decision not to go to Toronto at that time was that I had my work in Jerusalem, work which was so vital for getting me to think of the problems of others, not only of my own.

But above all, now in particular was the time when I needed to be alone to cry, to be miserable, to be able to grieve, without anyone around me. Misery needs no bed-fellows. I did not want to have to account to anyone for my red eyes, my restlessness, or my frequent recourse to the telephone. I wanted to be able to choose whether to eat or to skip a meal and, above all, when to let other people enter my life.

Hence, once the Toronto part of the family had left, about a week after the end of the *shiva*, I also declined to have anyone move into my apartment even for a trial period, as Alon had suggested. I knew that I would be able to handle being on my own and felt that this would not be qualitatively different from what I had experienced six years earlier, when Moshe remained in hospital for five months. Realizing how much I cherish my privacy, I was adamant in my refusal to have a flatmate. I preferred to have a trial period for living alone. It turned out to be an arrangement which suited me.

Salman Rushdie, the Anglo-Indian writer living in hiding because of the death sentence passed on him by Iranian Islamic fundamentalist, has said: "Our lives teach us who we are." What did my new life experiences teach me about myself? I do not tear out my hair, bite my nails or howl when I am miserable, but during the first two months after Moshe's death I often cried out of the blue. That is to say, I would suddenly dissolve into tears, while standing on line, waiting for a bus, or when listening to a choir sing "Miserere." Weeping at such times was always uncontrollable; I often found it most embarrassing, since it occurred in public, but there was nothing I could do to staunch the flow of my tears at such times. I could only try and get home as quickly as possible, so as to be on my own and unobserved by others. Nor could I have said whether I was weeping for Moshe or for myself on such occasions. All I knew was that I felt miserable and forlorn. Nothing that anyone could have said or done to me at those times would have made me feel less doleful and desolate about my life, bereft of him.

The English poet John Donne wrote: "Any man's death diminishes me." I wanted to add, "How much more so when the man was my husband," to those memorable words. My individual identity had been framed by being Moshe's wife, which included being *"Frau Professor,"* and I had derived much of my prized sense of self from it.

Helen Rose Fuchs Ebaugh, the American sociologist who studied the role of 'becoming an ex,' that is to say, the role of the divorcee, ex-nun or widow, was able to show that this is a role of transition, during the time when the 'ex' discovers and masters a new script with a new role. Once the transition is completed, other roles and different aspects of her identity take precedence. (Ebaugh,

1988). It was clear that I would have to learn to re-orient myself and, in time, to develop a new sense of myself.

From the start I tried to think of people who were worse off than myself, or of situations that could have been more wretched. Thus, the words of Erica, whose husband was seriously ill with cancer, rang in my ears: "One needs luck to die." Moshe had been lucky in so far as he did not suffer at the end, an end which was fortunately not too protracted but did give us enough time to get used to the idea of his dying.

As additional examples I felt that wives of husbands with Alzheimer's disease (I had several such friends) were tied to the living dead, who were unaware of their surroundings, yet needed constant care. The unfortunate spouse in such a couple was certain of only one fact: That the husband's or wife's state could not but deteriorate, and that there was no chance in a million for their improvement.

In short, I counted my blessings. For example, I imagined what might so easily have happened but, thank God, did not. What if Moshe had had his cardiac arrest on a plane to Toronto? After all, we had intended to visit our children there, two weeks later. I had visions of the plane being forced to land in Athens and an ambulance rushing Moshe to a hospital where no one understood anything but Greek, and where the medical services were such that he had no chance of recovering. (It is true that he did not recover in the Jerusalem hospital either, but at least we knew he had had the best medical care possible). Or worse still, if his heart had given out while he was driving a car, his cardiac arrest might have caused a major traffic accident with numerous fatalities. A scenario too horrible to contemplate.

These reflections made me appear to react strangely to all outward appearances, for instance when Adena, an old friend from Philadelphia, called me during the *shiva*.

"I am fortunate," I told her. "Moshe could have died on a plane or while driving a car."

She replied simply: "You are not fortunate."

After all, I had just lost my husband. Whom was I trying to fool about the impact of that loss? In hindsight I realized that I was trying to protect myself from my new, unbearable reality, trying to manage the unmanageable.

In spite of my bereavement, I was well aware of the benefits with which I was blessed: I have several trump cards, one of which is my good health, which enables me to live on my own and to have the energy for the kind of life I enjoy. Another, which is of no smaller value, is my very loving and caring family. No less crucial is the fact that I have work which is very meaningful to me and does not merely kill time. It is not only challenging but enables me to help others. By giving to my patients, I receive. They allow me to enter into their world, be it their country of origin, their profession, their particular life-style or their relationships, thereby enriching me. And of no small importance, they make me feel how crucial I am for them. This is of particular significance at a time when I have lost the person to whom I meant so much and who meant so much to me. And above all, my work gives structure to my life — I have to get up in the morning to see my patients. And while working I can forget my feelings of sadness and solitude, at least for a few hours of the day.

I have a comfortable home and was not left financially destitute by Moshe's death. And last but not least, I am not afraid to be on my own; I enjoy reading and listening to music, so that I never feel bored. And I have a telephone that connects me to all those people who are dear to me, especially to my children in Toronto. Soon after Moshe's death, I spent a few hours daily on the phone to contact all those people here and abroad who had known Moshe well. After the first few months I stopped being so dependent on these calls but made sure to talk to Jonathan and Yona at least once a week.

My grandchildren are an extra special gift. A note of warning is timely at this point: Like any grandmother I am totally objective about their attributes and qualities, enabling me to sing their praises unashamedly. My heart leaps with joy when I play hide-and-seek with the four year olds, Tal or Neri, and they keep on hiding in the same spot; when I listen to Elisha's jokes repeatedly and love how he laughs as he asks: "Why did the chicken cross the road?" again and again; when I hear Tal's voice on the phone from Toronto or when she spontaneously wraps up a flower which she has taken out of a vase and presents it to me as a gift on my visit to Canada; when four-year-old Neri struggles valiantly as he reads Dr. Seuss' book aloud to me in English; and when seven-and-a half year old Elisha defeats me in every game of Monopoly we play. The list of pleasures they bestow on me is inexhaustible, and I am forever grateful to their parents for having created such adorable brats.

> The first time I had to check "widow" on a form, I had to hold my hand because it started to shake. Until then I had avoided saying that word or even thinking of myself as a widow.
>
> Interviewee in Phyllis R. Silverman's *Widow to Widow* (1986).

Four and half months after Moshe's death, I flew to Canada and the United States, to see my children and friends. At Ben Gurion airport I was asked to fill out "Marital Status" on a form. I pretended not to understand what this meant at first. The "W" word "widow" is a harsh and cruel one and not one with which I wanted to be associated in any way. (Only later did I learn that the Latin word from which it is derived means "to be empty, deprived"). It was as if it stamped my new, and to me still unacceptable, reality, bestowing a finality on it.

For me, however, there is no absolute finality because Moshe continues to live on, in my thoughts. This means that there is, on one hand, the physical objective reality, according to which he is dead and buried. But there is also, on the other, a subjective mental reality, according to which I not only see him in my mind's eye during various parts of the day but also continue to perceive much daily life, including the people in it, through his eyes. Moreover, I hear his voice in my mind. So in a very real sense Moshe continues to be alive for me.[1,2]

I object to the designation 'widow' on other grounds also: Any name is a distinguishing mark, making it possible thereby to differentiate and to order. If we use the designation 'widow,' it distinguishes its bearers from non-widows. But this is a simplistic and false identification of the person thus designated, since this or any other name can never exhaust the identity of the person.

All this means is that I am not merely a widow but also a Jewess, a mother, a daughter, a psychologist, a friend, a writer, a grandmother, a tax-payer, a frequent traveler and a host of other designations.

There is yet another reason why I don't like to be identified as a widow over and above all the other possible identifications: 'Widow' implies loss. So whenever the word is used, it serves as a reminder of that loss, thereby rubbing salt into my wounds.

A similar issue applies to the adjectives that many people use when mentioning Moshe. They will not fail to add "late" when speaking about him ("your late husband") or even add, "of blessed

---

1. Marcel Proust's words are pertinent in this connection: "People do not die immediately for us but remain bottled in a sort of aura of life: As though they were traveling abroad."
2. Silverman and Nickman in *Continuing Bonds* (Klass et al., 1996): "Survivors hold the deceased in loving memory for long periods, often forever." (p. 349), and "The bond may shift so that it is not as central to life lived by the bereaved. The bond can take on a new form with time. But the connection is still there."

memory." Presumably they consider it as desecration of the dead to leave out these figures of speech. For me, they all serve as a constant reminder that Moshe has gone forever. But who wants or needs such reminders? Are not his empty bed, chair and closet sufficient?

I continued to talk in the royal plural for more than a year after Moshe's death; I used "we" freely, as if he were still around. Thus, I would invite a friend "to come and stay with *us*."

At the J.F.K. airport, the passport official asked me if I was by myself.

"You said we," he pointed out.

"I am sorry, but my husband died recently, so I still use *we*," I explained to him.

Eleven months after Moshe's death I wrote to friends: "We are expecting a Canadian grandchild." Even fifteen months after Moshe was gone — it was Channukah at the time — I said to a colleague: "I want to invite you to our candle-lighting."

It seems that all these situations had been so linked to Moshe in the past, that he was naturally included when they were mentioned. I had certainly not made a conscious decision to use the first person plural — it just came naturally to me. I do believe, however, that it was an unconscious outcome of my facing widowhood, one that resulted in making me feel that I had kept Moshe in my life.

With death I knew exactly where I was: It provided a finality. While I could imagine that Moshe was still around and might come in through the front-door at any moment, deep down I realized that he would never do so again. The finality meant that I could, after an interval, start my life again independently. This was music of the future but I was even then, in the first weeks of my grief, aware of its possibility.

Whenever death strikes, some families separate and become weaker, while others close ranks and grow stronger. I was fortunate that mine belonged to the latter category. I felt more connected to my sons and their wives than ever before. We all cared for each other and comforted one another in our major loss. I was sure the family would survive Moshe's death, with each of us eventually taking over different aspects of his functioning. Unwittingly I had stepped into his position as head of the family. But my sons were adults who each had his own family. They no longer needed me to help them make day-to-day or even important decisions. In fact, they were at my disposal to help *me* choose between my different options, for my man was gone, the person with whom I had discussed all matters of trivial or of vital importance. I would have to be careful not to allow myself to be parented by my children, since I was 'a big girl' now. But it was reassuring to know that they were able to help me not only in practical matters, but also to chew over problems whenever the need arose. And above all, I was certain of their unconditional love.

The day after *Yom Kippur* — the *shiva* having ended the previous day — I went to the bank with Jonathan (though I usually go to the bank by myself), in order to find out the state of my account and to order check books without Moshe's name on them. I also had to get a new health insurance policy — mine had been a joint one with Moshe. Meanwhile Yona looked over my financial papers in order to simplify the bookkeeping for me and to clarify my assets. I realized that I could never have handled these affairs on my own. Yona, being a highly competent lawyer, who specializes in tax matters, was the ideal person to do this chore for me.

More than a year later, I met Vera, whose husband Morris died when she was in her seventies. It was Morris who had looked after all the financial matters in their home, as she told me, adding: "I had never been inside a bank. I had never dispatched a letter. It was Morris who would write the address on the envelope and put a stamp on it. So I was totally lost when he died."

I was horrified at the helplessness in such everyday matters of this obviously capable, professional woman, and I responded in a way natural to me: "So you had a new challenge: To learn to cope with these prosaic, run-of-the-mill affairs."

"No," she protested, "I would like to set myself challenges and not to have them imposed on me."

I could see her point and sympathized with her and her newly imposed burdens. But the encounter with Vera highlighted for me the inordinate cost paid by widows in whose homes there had been a strict division of labor between husband and wife, as is often the case with people of my generation. (Among younger people, roles are usually less clearly defined and tend to merge). Had the wife died in such a family set-up, the husband would probably have been totally helpless concerning specific household chores. Thus, the loss of the marital partner, of either sex, would bring the total ignorance regarding very basic skills, of the spouse left behind, to the fore.

"I am quite unable to cook," a widower who was a physician, confessed to me recently. "My late wife completely took over that task."

"But you must have studied some chemistry," I argued, "surely that is far more difficult than throwing together a few ingredients and combining them into a meal."

The need here, however, was not only to acquire a new skill but also to adopt a different attitude which would proclaim: "Though I am a man, I am going to do the cooking"; or, in the case of the widow: "Despite the fact that I am a woman, I will attend to my money affairs."

Thank goodness I was not totally ignorant in money matters and certainly far from ignorant in secretarial ones. At an earlier stage of my life, before I had gone to university, I had trained to become a secretary, with the encouragement of my former high school principal, who thought this would be an appropriate career for me. Moreover, once I mastered the skill of driving, I also had to become acquainted with the garage that took care of the body of the car, another that repaired its electrical flaws and a third that fixed the carburetor. All these had been solely Moshe's responsibilities.

Even now, I still resent having to fix the car and to deal with tax and insurance matters. Yet there is also a part of me which is proud of my ability to do so.

But to return to the practical duties that were my lot once the *shiva* ended: There were many documents from official bodies that I had to obtain, among them a death certificate and an authorized will. Without these, no institution would pay out the life insurance or pension.

None of these activities fits in very well with mourning, geared as they are, to the nitty-gritty of daily life. It is money versus feelings, a rather harsh confrontation with objective reality. I had left many matters dealing with finances in Moshe's hands and he had handled them very ably. Now I would need help from my children to advise and check these matters for me.

Often widows are left with a great financial enigma: How to continue paying the mortgage on a widow's pension? Many of them have to move into smaller apartments. Thank God, the payment of the mortgage on our apartment had been completed many years ago, so I was extremely fortunate in not having to introduce far-reaching changes into my life in order to make ends meet. Thus, I was able to stay in my own apartment, which I love and which I shared with Moshe for thirty years.

Some of my widowed friends have to take in bed-and-breakfast guests in order to make ends meet. Such an arrangement has the advantage of preventing solitude; the woman does not need to eat breakfast on her own. Moreover, this setup creates an opportunity for her of meeting new people. I personally do not need anyone around me when I snatch a quick breakfast in the morning, before starting my work. But I admit that I lose out by not being able to meet new people that way.

Less than a month after Moshe's death, Alon raised the delicate topic of my buying the plot of land next to Moshe's grave. I am not superstitious by nature, so I did not fear that if I owned a specific grave, it might hasten the day on which I would need it. But my tendency is to withdraw from any preparation for my own death, as if I were light-years away from that scenario, so that there is absolutely no need to waste any time or thought on that topic. Looking at this avoidant behavior with the eyes of a psychologist, however, I can state unequivocally that this is a way of denying what awaits each and everyone of us.

An additional method by which I defend against the idea of my dying is by joking about it. Thus I argued with Alon: "Why should I care about what happens to my corpse? After all, I shan't be there to mind anything. Let them cart off my earthly remains to wherever they please." But Alon said quite simply: "It is for our sake that I make this request. We want to be able to visit your grave and that of dad at the same time, when the time comes."

I knew that unless I owned the plot of land next to Moshe's, the next Jerusalemite to die would be buried there. So I allowed myself to be swayed by Alon's argument.

When the two of us went to the Jerusalem Burial Society a couple of days later to make this purchase, we joked around. I doubt that many people go to that particular Society with any but a somber face.

I lived by the principle "Only do those things that you really want to do." Thus, when a neighbor invited me to a wedding at which I did not know anyone apart from those who had invited me, I realized that I would feel oppressed and miserable if I were to stay for the dinner and dancing. Therefore, after the religious ceremony, I excused myself with "I am in mourning" and escaped into the safety of my own home.

Did I experience Moshe's death as an 'appropriate' one? In other words, did I feel he was ready to die because he had lived a full life, which had reached completion? Though his life had been full almost to overflowing, it had by no means reached completion. I felt that he was called away too early from the party. How I wished we could have enjoyed old age together, delighting in our family and most especially taking pleasure in seeing our grandchildren grow up. Moshe did not even live to see Jonathan and Yona's little girl, born in March, 1993.

While I wanted to get on with my life within a month of Moshe's death, I tried to make sure that his projects were brought to completion. I also sought out his friends and colleagues who knew him and could talk about him to me. Above all, I did my best to carry on life as we had lived it together, upholding the same traditions, cultivating the same friends (as far as this was possible) and pursuing the same leisure activities. (It certainly brings to mind the play *Hamlet*, without the Prince of Denmark). But very gradually changes were introduced: New friends appeared on the scene, my children assumed more responsible roles within the larger family, at times substituting for their father, and I felt more independent.

In the work area, Moshe had headed several projects, among them a large dictionary of Modern Hebrew, a modern Arabic-Hebrew dictionary and a scientific edition of the book of Isaiah. He had not been able to finish any of these projects, nor had he completed his Jewish Biblical Theology, his History of Hebraic Studies in Renaissance times, and his Modern Hebrew Grammar.

Yet not only had he published numerous books and articles in the field of Bible and Semitic languages, many of which had become standard works, but he had also brought out a facsimile edition of the world-famous Aleppo Codex, the oldest and most exact manuscript of the complete Bible. To top it all, he had been awarded the prestigious Israel Prize, the highest honor the State of Israel can bestow on its citizens, for his scholarly accomplishments. We used to kid him that his many unfinished projects were a guarantee for long life. His puckish sense of humor allowed him to rejoice at the amount of work he was leaving behind for those who followed in his footsteps. His students and colleagues knew that he was irreplaceable, due to the breadth of his scholarly interests and the depth of his learning.

What happened to Moshe was wonderfully expressed in *Ecclesiastes* 2:18ff:

> I must leave it (my labor) to the man who shall come after me. And who knows whether he will be a wise man or a fool? Yet shall he have rule over all my labor in which I have labored, and in which I have shown myself wise 'under the sun'... For there is a man whose labor is with wisdom, and with knowledge, and with skill; yet he must leave it for a portion to a man who has not labored in it.

What happens when a man dies, leaving behind several uncompleted books and projects? To what extent ought his family to commit itself to having them completed and published? This is the question we were faced with after Moshe's death. I certainly wanted to see as many of his works as possible in print, because I knew that they were of high quality and would be valuable to his colleagues. But above all, this is surely what Moshe would have wanted, since he had put so much of his energy into these works.

Alon, who was closest to Moshe's subjects of interest, naturally stepped into the role of the executor of Moshe's unfinished works.

He handed them over to Moshe's colleagues and assistants for evaluation and advice and then discussed their findings and suggestions with them. But there were so many incomplete works that he needed time to deal with each and everyone of them. Yet Alon had very little spare time, busy as he was with his own teaching at Tel Aviv University, his writing in the field of religion and theology, and his own family.

Fifteen months after Moshe's death, Shraga, Moshe's trusted assistant, who had examined the manuscript of one of Moshe's projects, the Modern Hebrew Grammar on which Moshe had worked for a German publisher, determined that it was seventy percent complete. Alon volunteered to find an Israeli scholar who would add the missing thirty percent. But by then, the publisher had already handed over the commission for such a Grammar to another scholar. I was desolate; clearly Moshe had invested his thoughts and energy in vain. If only Alon had acted more quickly! Alon, however, did not share my feelings.

"Dad has left behind so many books and articles which were much closer to his heart," he said. "After all, he could never turn down any offer. Now we all have to realize that he is dead and that I have to look after my own career as well."

His words pained me when I first heard them, but thinking them over, I perceived that he was right. I could not reasonably expect him to sacrifice even more of his time on the altar of his father's career, extended beyond the grave. Yet I have to admit that a part of me wished that he could have done so.

I was reminded of Ruth, an American psychiatrist friend of mine, who had looked after her father's estate after he died. She discovered that he had kept a journal of all the patients he had treated in his New York office for close to forty years. What a fascinating fund of historical, medical and social information! But if Ruth had taken time out from her own flourishing career, in order to write his material up and have it published, it would have had to be at the expense of her own work, which was very important to her. Reluctantly, therefore, she turned down the idea.

The naked and unpalatable truth is that the needs of the living have to take precedence over those of the dead.

I felt sad when Nahum, a friend and colleague of Moshe's, told me that Moshe had been accepted at the Annenberg Center in Philadelphia for what would have been his last sabbatical before his retirement. "They would have considered it an honor to have Moshe there," Nahum added. Moshe had so much looked forward to a sabbatical year in which he would not have to teach but could devote himself entirely to completing several of his books.

Only the thought that Moshe might have died in Philadelphia, far from home, brought me back to the harsh reality.

Hillel, an old friend, who had lost his wife a few months earlier, called me up one day, with the following advice: "Don't make any changes during the first year after Moshe's death." I realized how important Hillel's advice had been only about a year later, when I read Lynn Cain's *Widow*. Lynn Caine was the young mother of two small children when her husband died of cancer. Believing that she would be better off near her two closest friends, she moved from her Manhattan apartment to a house in Hackensack, New Jersey soon thereafter. As she related it, she knew as soon as the moving van had left that she had made a terrible mistake. Her best friends had their own lives to live, and she felt let down and angry with them, very much alone and... crazy. Moreover, she had no social life in her new environment, after having cut herself off from everything and everyone she loved. Finally, a year later, she decided to return to the city where she felt at home.

I was spared these violent feelings by staying put, and by introducing changes into my life only very gradually. Hillel's advice was well taken, especially where my lifestyle was concerned. Thus, I had always enjoyed hosting my family and friends. My children from Toronto remained with me during the week of the Jewish festival of *Succoth* (Tabernacles) which occurred just after the *shiva*. Alon and his family and my uncle Werner joined them for many meals. The opportunity I had, to provide for my nearest and dearest, was the best antidote for grief.

Once the Torontonians had left, I invited friends over, especially for Sabbath meals. Here, Rebecca, a widow of several years' standing, served as my negative model. She told me that, after her husband's death, she never invited anyone but her family to her home. On further inquiry it transpired that she received only a few dinner invitations, eating most Sabbath meals by herself. This, I realized, was the consequence of her keeping to herself, a kind of 'solitary confinement.' I had no intention to limit my social contacts to those occasions when I was invited out, realizing that such invitations would quickly dwindle to nothing unless they remained reciprocal. I am aware, of course, that I was thereby trying to keep "business as usual," to preserve old routines, as in days gone by. It was a kind of holding on to my life with Moshe, perhaps even a denial that "things ain't what they used to be."

I did not want to postpone confronting the most necessary material changes for any period of time. Thus, I decided to change the carpet in what was now *my* bedroom, since I did not wish to look at the large blood-stain on it whenever I entered the room.

I wanted Alon and Jonathan to have as many of Moshe's belongings as they could use. This was the beginning of making Moshe's death more concrete for me. I realized it would be very painful and that many widows postpone taking this step for a year or longer. Some never take it. After all, each suit, each coat, arouses associations — how and where Moshe had acquired it and on which occasions he had worn it: The silk suits, bought in Italy in 1958 when he was a Jewish consultant for Metro-Goldwyn-Mayer for the filming of *Ben Hur*; the suits, shirts and shoes, custom-made for him in Hong Kong in 1968 when we were on our way to a sabbatical in New York. The list was endless. Moshe had kept all the clothes he had acquired over the years — we used to laugh that it was a wrench for him to part even from his *Bar Mitzva* suit. Now I would have to give these clothes away. But not all at once and not right away. Actually, in spite of his carefully chosen suits and jackets, Moshe seldom looked elegant; his breast-pockets bulged with his wallets and his pants had every appearance of his having slept in them. He looked at himself in the mirror only on two occasions: When he bought new clothes and when he shaved. Otherwise he did not seem to care about his appearance except for dinner engagements, when he proudly sported a brown, green or navy blazer. Then he would be receptive to compliments about the way he had dressed.

Before Jonathan returned to Toronto, I gave him the raincoat that Moshe had bought himself in Oxford, on his last trip to England, in the summer before he died. With great physical effort he had gone by himself to the local Marks and Spencer store and had picked a very handsome brown raincoat. I remember asking him how much it had cost, and he had shown me the receipt — unfortunately he could no longer remember sums of money recently spent — one of the lingering outcomes of his protracted coma. Moshe had never had a chance to wear it. Nor did it really fit Jonathan, who was much slimmer than Moshe had been. But I very much wanted this coat to remain in the family, even if it meant that it would have to be altered.

To Alon I gave Moshe's "Russian" fur cap and the snow-coat which he had acquired in New York. I had seen an advert in the New York Times in the winter of 1987 when we spent a year in Boston — it turned out to be Moshe's last sabbatical. The winter was a brutal one and Moshe needed a light, very warm coat. So on our next trip to New York, Moshe bought the gray down-filled cotton coat. (I remember his angry outbursts whenever I asked him to tie the belt.

He saw no need to do so — it was merely an onerous duty for him). Again it was important for me that his coat, also, be passed on to one of my sons, though I do not really know why I attached so much value to these coats over and above Moshe's other articles of clothing.

We also used to argue about his refusal to wear scarves — he had a selection of woolen and silk scarves, given to him by various relatives and friends, but he maintained that he could not wear them, that they all choked him. I claimed that without a scarf he would surely catch a cold, a fact he totally denied. He was probably right.

A year after Moshe's death, Tamara volunteered to go through his clothes with me, so that we could decide which of them to give away. I really felt that I had to confront the issue of parting with his clothes now, realizing that it would probably not be easier for me to do so at any later time. So why postpone the agony?

Many items remained for Alon and Jonathan to sort out themselves, in order to see if they could wear them. At that time Jonathan was in Israel with his family on vacation. Alon had not been able to make himself go through his father's clothes earlier, with the excuse that he was too busy. Moshe was several sizes larger than the boys, which constituted another good excuse for them not to deal with his clothes.

I decided to give most of the clothes which Alon and Jonathan did not take, to the store room established for the benefit of Russian immigrants. Since I went about it very practically and in stages, I did not find this operation too painful. I was very careful to avoid symbolic thinking of the kind: "I am emptying the house of Moshe's presence by this act." Instead, I pictured in my mind's eye how the Russian immigrants were enjoying the warm coats, suits, shirts, underwear and pullover that Moshe had chosen with such care. I reminded myself that at home they were unfortunately no longer of benefit to anyone. I had not looked at them daily, nor had I pretended that their owner was still around to wear them. In fact, I felt a certain sense of relief when this mission was accomplished.

One freezing day in winter, the local Arab street cleaner knocked at my door and asked me for a hot drink. His hands were quite red and raw from the cold, and so I decided to give him a pair of Moshe's warm leather gloves. I am sure that Moshe would have thoroughly approved.

A few special items remained, like Moshe's cuff-links (Alon and Jonathan do not wear shirts requiring their use). I decided to give these to close friends. One day I shall give away Moshe's ties. (My sons never wear ties). For some reason I have not parted with them yet. It is as if I needed to keep some small items of Moshe's wardrobe to myself, by holding onto them.

It required several months after Moshe's death for me to be able to dispose of other articles connected with him. I started with the X-rays of various parts of his body, which he had accumulated over the years. I also threw out the laboratory results of his blood, urine and stools. What purpose could they serve anyone now? None whatever, unless I considered bringing a malpractice suit, which I had no intention of doing.

At this stage I also invited the head librarian from an academic institution in Jerusalem to see if the library in which she worked might be interested in Moshe's Semitic books, that is to say, the Arabic, Syriac, Aramaic, Ugaritic, Ethiopic and Assyrian tomes, for which none of us had any use. We were interested in the Jewish section of the library only.

Alon found a student to transfer the card index of the library, which Moshe had accumulated for close to fifty years, onto sheets of paper, which he then Xeroxed and turned into a catalogue for university libraries and book stores abroad. (It took almost two years for this project to be completed).

I was going step by step: I finally gave away Moshe's canes for the handicapped to Barbara, Moshe's favorite physiotherapist, who knew patients who needed them urgently. Up to that point my grandchildren had played with them. The canes had always been their favorite toys.

The name-plate on my house-door remained as hitherto: Esther and Moshe Goshen-Gottstein.

Eleven months after Moshe's demise, his name is palpably absent from the new telephone directory. How did those who composed the directory find out? I had requested to be transferred to the digital system, which meant that my phone number would be changed. I was asked for my name and thoughtlessly failed to add Moshe's. So, inadvertently and without intention, his name is missing. The phone directory makes a kind of negative statement: Only my name appears next to my address and phone number. Moshe does not live on that page any longer. That is clear for all to see.

When my phone number was changed, Alon remarked: "Dad won't know our new number." He was obviously still in close contact with his father.

Moshe used to have a special parking place in front of our house, clearly designated by a handicapped sign painted on the stretch of road it occupied. About a year after his death, I noticed that this sign had become more and more imperceptible. In fact, it was barely visible, as if to symbolize Moshe's disappearance from this world. That was the way I interpreted it.

I continue to wear my engagement and wedding rings. It never occurred to me to do otherwise. They have become part of me, so why give them up now? I do know that Moshe is gone forever, but for thirty-eight years there was a joining between the two of us. In some sense we are still joined, since I carry what Joyce Brothers calls "this memory bank of marriage" inside me. (*Widowed*, p. 91.) This is what these rings symbolize. I suppose that if I would decide to remarry, for which I have definitely no desire at present, I would take off these rings. Stephanie Ericsson, in her book *Companion through the Darkness* (1993), adds a further reason for wearing the wedding ring:

> Wearing the ring is an important gesture. After all, we are not divorced! We did not choose to lose our spouses. We had no say in this event whatsoever. We were married and then we weren't. (p. 129)

I have meanwhile acquired a new video player and cable television (how Moshe would have loved these), and I have had to replace some of our thirty year-old shutters, but all the furniture remains in place. That includes his neglected bed, his night-table and chair.

I still feel as if I am opening closets not my own when I open those in Moshe's study. Even nine months after his death, I discovered hitherto unknown treasures he had accumulated, such as an envelope with coins from the different countries we had visited together: I had been totally unaware of their existence.

As for the hand-written lectures and articles that are still in the drawers almost two years after his death, sorting them out would necessitate my making the choice of what to keep and what to throw away. But as yet, I am unable to dispense with any of them.

After my great dream on the very day of Moshe's death, I secretly hoped to have many more dreams about Moshe, so that I might gain deeper understanding of what his life and death meant to me. Unfortunately, however, the dreams in which he appeared were few and far between. When he was in them, he was always the Moshe after his coma, that is to say, the new and different Moshe, far more fragile and vulnerable than before, and with specific handicaps.

Three and a half months after his death, I dreamed:

> Moshe is trying to talk to me across a room full of people

> but I cannot hear him. As he walks, I see him leaning over
> a cane. Later, in his bath, he suddenly turns white. Shall I
> call for help in the corridor or get help in some other way?
> I feel he is dying.

In the dream, I believe that Moshe is attempting to talk to me. This may be wishful thinking on my part. In any case, I am unable to hear him. Thinking about the dream, I wonder whether there is something deficient in me — my hearing — which prevents me from receiving his message. Or is it something inherent in the situation, "talking across a room full of people" who are surely not silent? It would be a mission impossible, like trying to talk across continents or worlds. So, irrespective of who is responsible, Moshe is no longer able to communicate with me. This is a fact which I will have to accept and to which I will have to reconcile myself.

Just like after his recovery from his coma, Moshe leans over his cane in the dream. Clearly, it is the damaged Moshe I see, one who could be struck down at any time.

The dream repeats his 'death' scene by re-enacting it in a new version. But the main ingredient remains: I am once again overwhelmed by helplessness, not even knowing where to run for assistance.

It seems that I have to relive the trauma of Moshe's end again and again, to experience a repetition of it in fantasy and dream, before I can 'digest' and assimilate it, since it was too disruptive and powerful an event for me to master at the time it occurred.

The next dream I can remember, in which Moshe appeared, occurred eleven months after his death:

> Moshe looks for a restaurant which will be suitable when
> Norbert comes. I protest and wonder why he did not book
> at a specific, good hotel. Moshe explains: "Because they
> don't serve sauce for gefilte fish." I consider his judgment
> to be poor — as if the sauce were a major consideration.

Again the dream seems to present Moshe in his post-comatose state when he suffered certain mental impairments, such as his inability to weigh up and judge a social situation. But am I not being judgmental, if not to say unnecessarily critical, of Moshe? It is true that Norbert is a very special friend of ours and that we want to take him out to a top quality eating-place. But is it really of such consequence whether we go with him to a restaurant or to a good hotel?

Moshe seems to concentrate on a minor detail of the menu, the sauce for the gefilte fish, and I resent this. But on the other hand, could it not signify also that Moshe takes care even of the smallest, least important details, so as to make sure that our friend will get the best treatment? Should that be so, I will have to re-evaluate Moshe's behavior in his last years of life, when I too easily dismissed what irritated me as due to the after-effects of his coma, thereby doing him an injustice. As I understand it, revision is the order of the day.

Only fifteen months after Moshe's demise did I remember another dream in which he figured:

> Moshe puts a wad of dollars into a secret compartment
> when someone, who is not a family member, is present.

Here Moshe is preparing a nest-egg for the family; but in Israel, at that time, it was a minor offense to keep dollars at home — one was obliged to deposit them in the bank after having returned from abroad.

Again Moshe's judgment seems to be poor, in the way he hides his money when others are present. But surely, the predominant factor here is his good, caring side, which plans for our future, possibly a future in which he will not participate. The dream does not tell us who the non-family member is. He might be a friend, in which case Moshe could not be faulted for hiding the money in his presence.

Am I once again jumping too quickly to the conclusion that Moshe's judgment is not the best? Is not this dream emphasizing Moshe's concern for his family, as it emphasized his concern for a close friend in the previous dream? Perhaps I did not give him sufficient credit for this when he was alive, focusing instead on what I took to be post-coma-related deficits. In that case, the dream may point out the need to redress the balance in Moshe's favor.

Moshe has been gone for more than a year. Yesterday an acquaintance whom I called up asked me how I was doing. For the first time I forgot what she was referring to and why she sounded concerned. I seem to have turned a corner; I no longer feel guilty if Moshe is not on my mind at all times of the day. Obviously I had felt the need to hold onto him by constantly thinking about him. Through what Dennis Klass calls this "continuing bond" with Moshe, I had been enabled to resolve my grief and to accept my new reality (Dennis Klass et al. [eds.], 1996). But at this point in time, I consider the obligation of keeping him constantly in my thoughts no longer appropriate. I cannot remain in perpetual mourning. I have to rebuild my life without him, hard as I know this will be. Life is too important for me to abandon it and merely to live in the past.

At times, special symbolic measures are required, to enable a woman to separate herself from her deceased husband. Muriel exemplifies this cogently: She is a family therapist whose husband Arthur had been a true partner in every aspect of her life, even treating couples together with her. Not surprisingly she was absolutely devastated when Arthur, on whom she had been so dependent, died. She was too depressed to reach out even to her friends. But when her birthday approached, close to the first anniversary of Arthur's death, she made the resolution that it was time to separate herself from him. As a first symbolic gesture she bought herself a new telephone, one that looked old-fashioned; it was white with gold trimmings, feminine, frivolous and a little kitschy, one that Arthur would never have bought her. In fact, he would probably have disapproved of it. The other telephones in their homes were all plain-looking and purely functional. Muriel found a place for this new phone on the table next to her husband's side of the bed, and was delighted to be able to use it.

Soon after Arthur's *Yahrzeit*, Muriel took a further step in the same direction: She bought herself a new car. Arthur had only bought second hand cars because new ones quickly depreciate in value and he was opposed to wasting money, although he had plenty of it. Muriel, on the other hand, did not care about money, as long as she had enough to live on.

Through her newly acquired telephone and car, Muriel was sending the message that she was ready to reach out to the world of her friends again. But of even greater importance was her implied statement that her values, needs and tastes were no longer necessarily identical with those of her husband. In short, she was differentiating herself from him on the way toward separating mentally from him. Rather than remaining inextricably fixated in a union with him — a union which now belonged to the past — she would henceforth be able to grow and develop, although Arthur would always remain an exceedingly important part of her mental interior.

Today I made space for myself on Moshe's desk and installed my newly acquired word processor there. I removed the articles that were published posthumously to a book-shelf. His desk and drawers are still full of his belongings. To me it feels as if I were dispossessing him at his desk, his holiest of holies. And to think I am doing it with a computer, from which he had always shied away! I could have installed it in his library, in the room next door, but fourteen months after Moshe's death, isn't it time that I no longer by-pass his desk and chair?

At first, I left the photos of the children and grandchildren, as well as those of his parents and myself, on top of his desk. But a week later I took them down. I have my own picture gallery, consisting of my grandchildren and Moshe, on the window-sill of the kitchen and on top of the television. But a large, black-framed photograph of Moshe now stands on top of his desk.

March 25, 1993. Eighteen months after Moshe's death, Jonathan calls me to say that Yona has gone into labor. I have the strong urge to share the news of this overwhelming event with Moshe. It is after all his grandchild who is about to be born, no less than mine, but it is the first grandchild without Moshe.

I wonder whether to visit Moshe's grave in order to communicate and to join with him in the celebration of this event. But if I did so, I would subscribe to the belief that he is alive in his place of burial. I have to remind myself that only his earthly remains are there. To be precise, he is alive only in my mind and in the mind of all who remember him.

Two days later, Jonathan calls to inform me of the name Yona and he have chosen for the baby: Ma'ayan, which is the Hebrew for a spring. He adds the following *midrashic* interpretation of this name:

The M stands for Moshe, whose name Pharaoh's daughter explained in the biblical book of *Exodus* in the following words: "Because I drew him out of the water" (she had found the wicker basket in which Moshe was hidden in the rushes by the river's brink). Through Ma'ayan's birth, Yona and Jonathan's baby had also been drawn "out of the water." The next three Hebrew letters make up the Hebrew word for "eye." Together, this combines to Moshe looking down at this little girl.

My heart jumps for joy that Moshe had been uppermost in their thoughts when they picked a name for their newborn daughter.

Climbing alone

Shall I compare my newly widowed state to walking through a wood, with its thickets and uncertain pathways leading to unpredictable and potentially dangerous places? I pray that the wood, filled with dread, be changed to one in which I may find solace and peace.

Perhaps, better still, to compare my state to that of a lone climber attempting to conquer Mount Everest. There is no one to shoulder the burden, yet there is the drive to keep climbing (though the footing is unsure and the elements bear down) and above all, to survive. There are the ropes for support — the family and friends — but if I fall, the pain and injury will be predominantly mine.

Ecclesiastes 4:9 has put it perfectly:

> Two are better than one. For if they fall, the one will lift
> up his fellow but woe to him that is alone when he falls;
> for he has not another to lift him up.

Aloneness, like a mosaic, is composed of a myriad trivial issues: You cannot request that someone get up from the table to bring you the salt. Nor is there anyone to help you look for your diary which you feel you cannot live without but which, after a prolonged search throughout the house, you have not found. The mailman cannot deliver the registered letter when you are out, and you have to make a special trip to the post office to pick it up. You yourself have to change the light bulbs and to take over the bookkeeping, to have the car fixed in the garage, to phone the insurance about it and to fill in the requisite forms. There is no one to close the buttons at the back of your dress. You cannot say: "Please fetch my shoes from the shoe-maker," or "do come home earlier to-day, so that you can open the door for the plumber" or even "please call up the accountant to answer some of his questions." There is no one to take your arm when you walk in the street, nor is there anyone to remind you to do any of the dozens of things which you have to accomplish in any one day. You are no longer on the mailing-list of cultural events, such as academic guest lectures, openings of exhibitions, centenary celebrations, related to your husband's place of work. You are also out of the mainstream of current thought about developments in the fields that interested him and which he used to talk about at home. All these and many, many more items you have to get used to or to tackle by yourself, whether you feel like it or not. You even have to go to weddings and funerals on your own.

What it amounts to is that you have to be totally self-reliant and maximally efficient, exploring your internal resources, with the realization that help can come only from within yourself. Decisions must be made by you alone and not by a committee of two. You have to be responsible for everything you do — you do not even have the luxury of blaming your life-partner for anything that goes wrong. Basically, all this implies that, without making more than the usual effort, you cannot have a life of quality.

Of course you could ask your children to help with some of these chores, but you know that once you give in to the temptation to request their help in running your daily life, there would be no end to this. Obviously they would resent such a state of affairs and thereby come to resent you.

The unshared chores are minor compared to the fact that there is no one to ask you on a regular basis: "How has your day been?" That covers the highs and lows, the excitements and the achievements, as well as the disappointments and the frustrations, and of course the latest gossip which adds spice to daily living — who married and who divorced, as well as the hatches and dispatches, not to mention the latest news of the university.

One of the saddest aspects of remaining alone is that you can no longer share your experiences as a matter of course. Often there are the humorous events that you want to savor with someone else, the private jokes you enjoyed, giggling together over the reviews of people and events: How Donald made a big deal of each dish that Bernice served (though she is a mediocre cook), or the story of the professor who wrote a book of explicit love poems. And to whom can you talk about a friend of old who suddenly reappeared in your life, looking a hundred years older? You come home from a conference, dying to share your impressions and experiences with someone, about the people you spoke to — whether they are old friends, your publisher, a literary critic or a writer — the lectures you heard, the ideas that were expounded. You'd give anything to laugh with someone about a certain exchange you had and to weigh up a certain suggestion with somebody. But you learn to keep all this to yourself since none of it is urgent enough to call up a friend.

> I shared everything that was difficult with him (Yitzhak Rabin, her husband) and remained with only half of it.
>
> Leah Rabin in a TV interview with Yael Dan, Jan. 7, 1996

There are many serious matters you are dying to share with someone, like those pertaining to your children and friends, one of whom had a recent cancer scare. And with whom can you share your joy in having helped an unnamed patient get over a difficult hurdle or the disappointment that another patient seems stuck? Last but not least, there are the upsetting incidents that you are desperate to confide in someone you can trust, as when I was interviewed on a television show and felt — wrongly, as it turned out — that I had bungled the interview. To whom could I run for comfort and reassurance? Finally, of course, it was Alon to whom I turned in my desperation, and he had the desired calming effect.

Above all, the private shorthand used by long-time couples, the secret language of marriage, that usually can't be shared by anyone else, can no longer be employed. Nor can the intimacy of non-verbal communications, with its exchanges of knowing glances, hinting at a shared assessment of other people and of what they said or did, be recaptured. Missing, too, are the little supportive gestures. In short, there is an intimacy deprivation.

With whom can you break your head over a predicament, or who can help you see a problem in your life with detachment? Who can serve as well-intentioned listener and critic to prevent you, for example, from exploding unnecessarily at someone you feel has slighted you? In short, you need a person close to you to restore your balance, and you feel you have lost the person who could moderate you. Moshe was always a good sounding-board; he was very level-headed and a surprisingly good natural psychologist.

There is no one to reassure you on a regular basis that you are a worthwhile, lovable person. Everyone doubts himself from time to time. This easily leads to feelings of depression and despondency. It is much harder to pull out of such negative states when you are alone and seemingly trapped in a one-way alley, with no alternative road in sight.

As Robert S. Weiss pointed out in *Going it Alone* (1979):

> Without an emotional partnership like that of marriage, intermittent loneliness appears nearly inescapable. (p. 192)

and

> Loneliness seems to occur regularly when emotional life is unshared. (p. 194)

There is nothing like a good argument with a worthy partner who takes a stand opposite to yours. With Moshe gone, most dialogues have to be conducted within myself, with me having to play devil's advocate against my own reasoning.

One fine day, I discovered with dismay that I was talking to myself. As I was making order among the dishes in the refrigerator, I heard myself saying aloud: "I don't need this tonight." Had I joined the ranks of the little old ladies we encounter in the street, who talk to themselves? The very idea made me shudder. I felt I had to investigate this problem further.

I had noticed that some women in my exercise class had the need to talk constantly, as they dressed or undressed, and even during the work-out. Was theirs a need to communicate or merely to hear their own voices? And did I kid myself when I claimed that I do not have such needs? Is it possible that I had a deeper need than I realized, and that this was expressed when I talked to myself?

I remember a former patient of mine, a single woman, who lived on her own. She kept a stuffed toy-animal on her couch with which she would hold long conversations. She was prevented from keeping a live dog, because she was out of the house most of the day. *Faute de mieux*, this was her way of pouring out her thoughts and feelings. I felt full of pity for her in her overwhelming loneliness and in her need to resort to such a basically frustrating measure in order to try to overcome it.

Marion, a divorced friend of mine, told me that when she was in the stages of separating from her husband, she would put the dog in the back-seat of her car and, while driving with him, would tell him all the awful things her husband had done to her that day. She just had to share this with some other living creature, to get it off her chest, irrespective of whether she was being understood or not.

I personally did not have this overwhelming need for a living creature with whom to share my innermost thoughts. My internal dialogues were conducted between me and my alter ego.

Several of my widowed friends have confided in me that whenever they have to make a difficult decision, they 'converse' with their late husbands about it. One particular widow, Natalie, told me that after she has solved a difficult problem, she will look skyward, to her late husband, and say proudly: "You see, I was able to do it."

I never behaved in this way. After Moshe died he was no longer a partner with whom I conversed. Perhaps I am too much of a realist.

Young children, as we know from Piaget, the developmental Swiss psychologist, hold monologues, even when playing with other children. They talk to themselves as though they were thinking aloud. The outsider is expected neither to attend nor to understand. The point of view of the other person is never taken into account. Even when alone, the children go on announcing what they are going to do. This type of speech precedes their social talk with others. (J. Piaget, 1932)

I realize that often there is no one for me to talk to but myself, yet most of my conversations are conducted in my head in the form of internal arguments or thoughts. Of this I am certain. So why did I talk aloud to myself? I decided to carry out a small research project on myself and to write down every verbal utterance I voiced, in order to examine the nature of these utterances.

I learned to my amazement that most of my utterances were in German. German is my mother tongue, but I left Germany at the age of ten, spent a year in Engelberg, Switzerland, and lived in England during the following fifteen years; these included World War II. During that war, German was regarded as the enemy tongue, and we were actively discouraged from speaking it, especially in public places. However, I moved to Israel a year after marrying Moshe, whose mother-tongue was also German. For him German had remained alive not only because he was three years older than I when he emigrated, but also because his parents never learned to speak Hebrew. Moshe had lived in England for only one year, which he spent in Oxford, for his post-doctoral work. When I moved to Jerusalem, the two of us spoke mostly English together, with a liberal sprinkling of German. In fact, my German was revived in Israel, helped by the fact that my first Israeli analyst, Dr. Erich Neumann, was also German-speaking, so that my analysis was conducted in German.

Now I discovered that, although I believed that the language in which I was most fluent and in which I conducted my thinking was English, German, which I had acquired prior to English, predominated on very specific occasions.

Only a quarter of my utterances were in English and only five percent were in Hebrew. Hebrew as a spoken language was the last language I acquired (in between I had learned French at school), and hence it hardly figured in these murmerings.

What was the content of these self-addressed remarks? By far the largest proportion of them, thirty five percent, was in the nature of a running commentary, sometimes whispered, as if I wanted to inform myself about my own activities. For example, *"Das Licht hab ich noch nicht angemacht,"* i.e. "I haven't switched the light on yet." It was all on a very humdrum level.

Fifteen percent of my utterances centered on my inability to find a certain object and were often in the form of questions. Thus, *"Wo hab ich denn meinen Schlüssel?"* i.e., "Where is my key?"

I also discovered that I was giving instructions to myself about what to do next in ten percent of the instances. For example, *"Jetzt will ich noch die Melone schneiden,"* i.e. "Now I still want to cut the melon."

Ten percent of my verbal expressions were exclamations of surprise: *"Um Gotteswillen,"* i.e. "For God's sake" — when I found ants in my kitchen or when, while driving, I saw my car-mirror was tilted to the side, so that I could not see the cars behind me. Such exclamations could occur in English and Hebrew as well.

I tended to be judgmental about myself and even give myself a bad name in ten percent of these murmurings. For instance, *"Das war nicht gut,"* i.e. "That was not good," when I drove onto the curb while turning a corner, or when I failed to notice a car entering my path. Occasionally I called myself derogatory names like "idiot" as when I put away my keys before I had locked the car. Or worse: *"Ich bin ja verrückt geworden,"* i.e. "I have gone out of my mind," when I put on my clothes instead of my bathing-suit. The attribution of craziness was not confined to myself. *"Ist der verrückt geworden?"* i.e., "Has he gone crazy?" was my reaction to a car turning round in the midst of a busy street.

On certain occasions I also had recourse to expletives which tended to be in English. Thus, when I looked for my pen, I vented my negative feelings with: "Where the bleeding hell?" The name calling and expletives amounted to ten percent of all my self-addressed utterances. The latter were not always completed. Often it seemed sufficient for me to exclaim: "Where the...?" which stood for "Where the hell is my car?" Other utterances also remained incomplete.

It seems then that all my verbal, self-addressed utterances centered around my home, my office or my car — an extension of my home. They never appeared regarding any members of my family, my friends, my work or my other interests. Certainly Moshe did not figure in any of them. I feel certain that I voiced such utterances already when Moshe was still alive, but then I paid no attention to them. Only now, when I feared that they portended a decline in me, did I pay attention to them. My guess is that everyone, to a smaller or larger degree, talks to himself or herself in these or similar circumstances, which do not depend on the fact that the speaker lives alone. I cannot say whether I voice my thoughts more frequently now than I did before Moshe died, but I am relieved to discover that talking to myself is not a negative sign of a change for the worse in me. Instead, it appears to be a universal human phenomenon. How easy it is, when living on one's own, to interpret one's actions in an uncomplimentary manner, since there is noone to give an objective judgment!

Did you know that when hens, which have just eaten to satiety on their own, are brought together with hungry hens, that are in the process of eating, the satiated hens will start to eat again? Appetite is obviously contagious, not only among hens but also among humans. This raises the question why some people, who live alone, such as the widowed, are prone to over-eating. It seems that the loss they have sustained, the emptiness in their lives, is expressed by them as physical hunger which no amount of food can satisfy.

I have to fight a tendency to nibble constantly; I must limit the number of cookies I eat in between meals and confine my food intake to breakfast, lunch and dinner. Usually I succeed, in spite of the fact that my desk is in the kitchen. A minor triumph.

There are people, however, who, when alone and depressed, do not eat at all. They have no appetite and may complain of an inability to swallow. That happened to me only in the acute phase of Moshe's hospitalization, especially in its beginning. At that time I took all my nourishment in liquid form. Joyce Brothers talks of a "grief diet," which causes immediate loss of appetite (*Widowed*," *op. cit.*, p. 114). How right she is!

Living by myself could have meant that I would be enveloped by silence. But I am a classical music fan, and in Israel we have a radio station called "The Voice Of Music" which operates from 6 a.m. until midnight. Having this station in the background makes my home feel alive in a good way and takes away the feeling of emptiness. I know a widow who, for the same reason, switches on the television when she enters her empty apartment.

What are the most important technological appliances in this modern age for widows, widowers, divorcees and singles? Not the word processor, the fax machine or the microwave oven, but the telephone and the answering machine. The former enables one to keep in touch with near and far-away friends and relatives. The latter allows one to go out without having to regret not being at home for incoming calls.

How did people who lived on their own in previous centuries, ever manage before the invention of the telephone? I know that they wrote and received letters, sometimes even on a daily basis from the same person. But the very possibility to hear the voice of someone special over the phone, and to gauge his or her mood from it, is invaluable. Such a person may even be able to humor one, to dispel the depression and to make the sun shine again, for however short a time. One does not even need to get dressed, comb one's hair or apply lipstick for the occasion. In fact, one can be woken out of one's sleep, to hear someone very dear on the other side. And if one feels like crying over the phone, no one will see one's distraught, red-eyed face. Thank the Lord for the existence of the telephone!

At times I feel as if I were shipwrecked and the sole inhabitant of an island. Now and again I leave the island and cross the bridge onto the mainland, or people from surrounding islands come to visit me. But, oh, so often, the bridge seems to have disappeared, enveloped by a thick fog. At such times, seemingly endless, my little island has to suffice me for better or worse, until, miraculously, the fog lifts and contact with people from afar, can be resumed. Am I destined to remain the sole inhabitant of the island?

I do feel alone. That statement seems too obvious to be made. Yet it has to be spelled out. The reality is that no friend is close enough to me to change that basic feeling. Perhaps I should say 'basic fact.' I see people most of the day, but when they have all left and I am not too exhausted, the feeling of loneliness overwhelms me. I yearn to share some of the happenings and thoughts I had during the day. On my own, there seems little sense or meaning to anything. It is like the sound of one hand clapping — something essential is lacking.

Stephan George, the German poet, writing about Nietzsche's death, speaks of "crying out with the pain of solitude."

Und aufzuschrein im Schmerz der Einsamkeit.

At times, a deep yearning for physical closeness, for intimacy, for someone into whom I can melt, overtakes me, a yearning so powerful that it really hurts. This craving through absence is like Hagar's unquenchable thirst because there is no drinking water anywhere in sight. Will a new source ever again appear before me? There are days of acute pain and perseverating thoughts, especially when I am not working at week-ends. My imagination conjures up scenes of chance encounters with fascinating men, old in experience but young in spirit. Yet fantasy cannot satisfy the thirst for long.

The most graphic description of such longing, focused on a particular man, was sent to me by my Bostonian friend, Daphne, a widow of two year's duration:

> A black depression descended over me. I am overwhelmed, nay flooded by it. What set it off? During the past weeks it was a letter that did not arrive. Was it due to a hiding of his face, as the Bible puts it when it means the withdrawal of God's favor: In short, a rejection? To-day it is the letter that did arrive but did not

live up to my expectations. I had exposed my innermost thoughts, the depth of my soul, to an old friend who only by innuendo related to the issues I had raised. He had his own agenda. Not his own problems, which I would willingly have heard about, but more weighty ones: The geo-political situation of the world, the forthcoming elections and the state of religion. I wanted something more personal, that could not have been published in Newsweek or the Times. My emotional hunger, though whetted, was not satisfied. The food I was offered made me more hungry than before and also very upset.

I recently met a widow who considered a permanent liaison with almost any man, in order not to have to face the empty home. Fortunately I have never felt so achingly lonely as to contemplate taking a similar step. I cannot think of a worse solution to the problem of solitude — in my case, joining with a man who does not live up to my needs and expectations would certainly lead to a terrible feeling of isolation.

Both my sons announced to me, unasked, that they would not stand in my way if I ever wanted to remarry. But I cannot even envisage the man who would attract me, share my interests and be warm, sensitive, witty, intellectually stimulating and able to rekindle my passion. I realize that my order is so tall that it cannot be met, especially at my age, when the choice of available men is constantly shrinking. Maybe I purposely set my aspirations so high that I will never have to give up my independence or feel the need to compromise. The fantasy of self-sufficiency, the safety of solipsism. I lead a very full life without being married, and I refuse to become what Irving Howe calls "a connoisseur of disappointment." But obviously many women handle this issue differently. There is no right or wrong way in this, since every person has different needs which demand different solutions. I speak only for myself.

People use each other
as a healing for their pain. They put each other
on their existential wounds.

Yehuda Amichai, *Love Poems*, p. 76

Karen, one of my American friends, was happy to have her ninety-year-old mother move in with her, after her husband died. She was glad to have someone whom she could care for and with whom she was able to share some of her activities. I think this was a successful kind of bridging. By the time her mother died, a few years later, Karen was able to make a life on her own.

I am fortunate to be able to call on my children when I must unburden myself to someone trustworthy, understanding and warm. Since both Alon and Tamara, who fit this bill, are extremely busy people, I try not to impose on them unless I am about to explode. They are both excellent listeners and intuit when I am in trouble. Alon is a born psychologist with a sense of humor, qualities that help dissipate my anxieties or depressive feelings when I do turn to him. But I can't call them to share the anecdotes heard at a meeting of friends the previous evening, or to tell them about the typical and peculiar behavior of one or other of the participants. I can make a general statement: "The talk was interesting," but why bother them with the details when they have their own large circle of friends? Yet it is the details that count for me.

I can also call on certain friends, but all these possibilities have their built-in limitations.

Oh, for the good old days when I was in analysis and could unload my innermost thoughts in relation to the most trivial or weighty events of the day! Oh, for the luxury of having set times during the week when I knew I would be heard by a sensitive person who would reflect back to me what I dimly realized but could not quite grasp! How I miss the mirror that was held up to me by the wise therapist. The mirror that I now hold up to myself is not of the same clear glass; it has many imperfections.

Those deeply committed to religion can communicate with God. Thus, Sister Maria Yeshua from St. Clare's Monastery, Jerusalem, said in a *Jerusalem Post Magazine* interview, published April 9, 1993:

> In prayer you can tell God all your hopes, questions. It's like talking to a friend, very intimate.

For a person like myself, who does not have this easy access to God, this seems an enviable state. Yet even Sister Maria admits:

> The truth is that sometimes — this happens when I am sad or tired — I think that if I had someone, flesh and blood, to be with, to touch, to hold, this could make life easier.

I did keep a journal during the first year after Moshe's death.[1] This was a wonderful way of reliving my experiences and of getting some distance from them. Distance is well-known to give enchantment, as the Queen of England recently said. The journal was also a way of confessing myself to myself, hoping that the thoughts on paper would allow me to see myself in perspective. Frequently, re-reading what I wrote days before, fertilized my mental apparatus; new ideas occurred to me and they joined the ranks of the other notes on the page.

It was with this journal that I could also share my feelings, irrespective of whether they were as miserable as hell or as joyous as Eden. Into it I could pour myself with impunity. Admittedly there was no feed-back from it, no encouragement, no reflections, no criticism and no advice, but it served as a kind of container for my thoughts and emotions. By transferring them from inside myself

---

1. One of Marta Felber's chapters of guidance after the death of a spouse is entitled: "Start a Journal."

onto the paper, I emptied myself of them. Simply put, writing helped me; many a time I ran to my journal like a drowning woman clutching at a raft.

If you were a banker, would you advise your client to invest all his or her savings in one particular stock? Surely you would consider that as unpardonable risk-taking, for if that stock crashed, all his or her savings would go down the drain.

That is the inherent weakness of monogamy: We choose the best marital partner possible and invest exclusively in him or her. But when we lose this exclusive partner, we are exposed to unspeakable grief, indescribable loneliness and a feeling of complete abandonment. His or her death leaves a veritable black hole in our lives.

No wonder that many people, especially those who lost one parent in their childhood and witnessed the shattering effects on the remaining parent, decide, perhaps not even consciously, never to undergo such an ordeal themselves. Though married, they form one or more significant attachments outside the marriage with members of the opposite sex, as an emotional insurance policy. Society may criticize them for this behavior which, if discovered, causes great pain to the marriage partner and may even lead to the break up of the marriage. This then is the paradox: While the person who forms such extra-marital attachments may be striving desperately to prevent having to lose the significant other, his or her behavior may lead to that very outcome.

Moshe, as a handicapped person ever since his by-pass surgery, made many demands on me. He needed me desperately for both mental and physical support, for solving his innumerable practical problems, for making decisions, for initiating social contacts, for organizing his journeys and even for packing his suitcases. The family joke relates how I had married Moshe because I was unable to pack suitcases whereas he was an expert at it. (The joke omitted to mention that packing time was always one of frayed nerves, a time when Moshe easily exploded). After his coma, the tables had been turned and he could only decide what to take on a journey — he could no longer arrange these articles in a suitcase. This had now become my task. It was hard for him to admit how vital I was for him at that stage of his life. As it was, his dependency was humiliating enough for this previously independent person.

I would be less than honest, were I not to admit that there were times when I bridled at the extent of Moshe's dependence on me. At such times, I was not as supportive as I should have been, but then I never set out to be an angel.

On the other hand, due to his handicap, Moshe had enjoyed several privileges from which I also benefited. Thus, he could park in many places where ordinary mortals had no such permission. He was also provided with a wheelchair at the airport and a steward who pushed it, enabling both of us to go to the upper floor by special elevator. The steward would then take us through the passport formalities without our having to stand on line. Arrived at our destination, another steward, equipped with a wheelchair, awaited us and helped us procure and carry the luggage through Customs. I had become used to this special treatment, feeling entitled to it. But now I was left to my own devices at every airport: I had to stand in line like everyone else and to carry my heavy suitcases unaided. And as for parking the car, I had to cruise around the area until I found a suitable spot.

I can see nothing reprehensible about going to the movies by myself, if I want to see a particular film and my friends have either seen it already or are busy when I am free. That happened to me when Zefirelli's *Hamlet* was showing. My friend Joyce called me up, praising this production. She added that only one other couple had been in the large Edison cinema when she and her husband had seen the film. From this I concluded that *Hamlet* would not be shown the following week. I called up a couple of friends to ask if they would like to join me. No one was free that evening; so I went off on my own.

I am not at a stage of life when I need to feel ashamed about going to public places of entertainment by myself, nor do I have to prove anything to anyone. And it is not as if I can enjoy a film only if I can discuss it later with the person who accompanied me. Of course it is more fun to share the experience and to argue about fine points of acting or directing. But even if something gets lost that way, the film itself is worth seeing when I am unaccompanied — better half an apple than none at all. In point of fact, I had to re-educate myself and change my attitude to what used to be partly, at least, a social experience and had now become a solitary one. In any case, going to the movies is not primarily a social event. Were it so, there would be no demand for home-movies which are frequently viewed by people on their own.

Moshe had a second cousin, widowed for ten years, who refused on principle to go to a cinema, theater or concert by herself, with the result that she hardly ever goes to the entertainment they provide, preferring instead to spend her leisure time in front of the television. I cannot think of anything sadder; yet, she argues, it would depress her immensely to go unaccompanied to a place of amusement where she is surrounded by couples. She has only a limited number of friends on whom she can call, and they likewise tend to stay at home, alone.

I have treated several young, unmarried women who declared that they would rather be seen dead than appear on their own at a cinema or theater. For them to be seen unaccompanied at such places meant going public about the fact that they had no boy-friend, a fact of which they felt ashamed. Hence they wanted to hide it. They were usually unaware that by going out alone, they exposed themselves to meeting new people, while staying at home deprived them of this opportunity.

Man is a creature of habit. Thus, I became used to walking home by myself even late at night — after all, Jerusalem is considered to be a safe city. So when an American colleague, who was invited with me to a dinner at friends, insisted on seeing me home afterwards, believing it to be undesirable for me to have to go home alone, I had to remind myself why he was concerned on my behalf. For me it was the most natural thing in the world to walk unaccompanied at any time of day or night. I had learned to accept it and no longer resented it after about a year had elapsed since Moshe's death.

"Don't leave everything to chance." This has become my motto ever since I have lived alone. I applied it to my approaching birthday, the first one without Moshe. I saw no particular virtue in turning this day merely into a day of remembrances and thereby a day of suffering for myself. So I decided to strike preemptively.

The birthday was to fall on *Shavuot* (Pentecost), the festival after Passover. I realized that Alon and his family would be tied up with the group of immigrant Rumanians, whom they had taken under their wings, for a good part of the day, though they were also going to have a meal at my place. In order to prevent any feelings of disappointment and discontent during the rest of the day, I invited people I really like, after dropping them a hint about my forthcoming birthday. I was delighted to receive flowers and other gifts from these friends who, I felt, were trying to make up for Moshe's absence. Maybe that was just my imagination, but it certainly helped me not to feel downhearted and desolate on "my" day, which could so easily have turned into a day of sorrow and sadness. I was proud of myself for having defused this particular bomb before it exploded.

The Jewish Sages said: "Who is wise? He who can foresee events."

Orna, a former patient, called me during the "great snow," when anyone who could stay indoors did so. She is a divorcee of many years standing and needed contact, feeling terribly lonely and cut off. I reminded her that we were lucky to have light and heat, the radio and television and above all, the telephone.

Is loneliness the same for the divorced as for the widowed? I wondered afterwards. Perhaps the crucial difference between us was that Orna had been more than a decade younger than I when she parted from her husband and therefore had reasonable expectations of finding another man, one to whom she could give and from whom she could receive. Though she had tried very hard to realize her hopes, her efforts had not been crowned with success. I had no such aspirations and was determined to build my new life, making it as gratifying as possible without a life-partner.

Solitude is certainly not the monopoly of the widowed, divorced and singles. I am only too aware that when a marriage dies, it can bind people in states of terrible isolation, with neither partner ever feeling, understanding or being sympathetic to the other, everyone being trapped within his or her loneliness. This is what Robert S. Weiss calls an "empty shell" marriage. (1973). Weiss points out:

> It is not marriage which is critical in fending off the loneliness of emotional isolation but rather the availability of emotional attachment, of a relationship with another person who promotes feelings of security and well being. It is attachment rather than marriage that is the issue. (p. 91)

During the first year of my widowhood I became aware of several uncontrolled, though unsubstantiated, fears which may rear their ugly heads and, at times, even turn into panic, when one lives alone:

About six months after Moshe's death, I opened my front door, ready to go to my office downstairs. Seeing that mail had been delivered, I ran down a few steps to take it out of the box. I was now so absorbed in who had written to me that I completely forgot about the unlocked front door. I took the mail with me and went down to my office.

Two hours later, as I came up to my apartment, I was appalled to see my front-door not only unlocked but open. Who had broken the lock and entered? I called out in terror: "Is anyone there?" but gradually managed to calm myself by reconstructing mentally what had happened before I saw my patients.

Ninety minutes later, as I was preparing to receive visitors and tried to switch on the light in the living room, total darkness descended on the apartment. Worse was to follow: The bell rang and I went to open the front door but found it locked. How could this be? After all, I never lock my front door from the inside with a key — I bolt it instead. Had a thief entered earlier, hidden in one of my rooms, played with the electricity and mysteriously locked my front door? I had no answer to any of these questions.

I welcomed my guests, whom I had not seen for a year, by sharing my consternation and fears with them. Only then did common sense prevail: I went to the electricity box and discovered there had been a short circuit which I was able to repair at once. Could there be an alternate explanation for the locked door as well? While talking to my visitors, I ruminated about this. Then suddenly it came to me: Since I had earlier become aware of the fact that I had forgotten to lock the front door when I went down to my office, I must subconsciously have tried to make up for this oversight by locking it from the inside.

"Think of an alternative for your fear!" That would have to be my motto in the future in order to prevent myself from panicking and suspecting the worst.

Its first application: Raindrops are falling heavily on the terrace outside my bedroom. They sound like footsteps. I have to remind myself that they only sound like them, they are not such. No one has entered my terrace, nor has anyone come into my apartment when I hear noises. I need to remember at such times that my front door is bolted and that my windows have iron bars in front of them. So no one could possible enter without my permission.

Yet I did realize that I could not relinquish my vigilance altogether for any suspicious noises or smells — of gas or fire — since I needed to forestall real dangers. After all, nobody else would be on the alert for such signals.

Finally, what I feared really came to pass — or so it seemed: Somebody did try to break into my apartment. It happened in broad daylight. I was out for just over an hour and on my return, when I tried to open my front-door, the key did not fit into the lock which had clearly been tampered with. I felt compelled to share these events with someone close to me and therefore called Tamara to release the tension by talking about this traumatic experience and... went to my Tuesday morning seminar at the university which I would not miss for anything. Back home, I phoned Alon who informed the insurance people and also obtained the phone number of the company that forces doors open in such circumstances. Fortunately my office is in the same building as my apartment, so I was able to make phone calls from there. A representative of the company appeared within half an hour and broke the lock of my front door, enabling me to enter my apartment.

Everything passed without panic — I had rehearsed similar scenes too many times in my mind to be overthrown by the event when it actually occurred. I considered myself really lucky that the burglar had been unable to get into my apartment and wreak havoc in it and .... of course also, that I had not lost my head.

P.S. The mystery was solved later: A new neighbor in the building mistook my front-door for that of the cellar, trying to force it open. But at least it is reassuring to know that no one attempted to burgle my home in broad daylight.

The horror of serious illness. How will I cope with it if I am alone? As I contemplate the fearful possibility, I feel strange sensations in my right hand. Are these the first signs of a stroke? I try to move the fingers of that hand. No problems there. But now a new worry overtakes me: Would I be able to reach my children at night, would they hear and answer my phone call? Perhaps I should not bolt my front-door at night, only lock it from the inside. At this point the strange sensation has mysteriously passed into my left hand. Perhaps these are the messengers of a degenerative muscular disease.

One part of me steps back and laughs. I really do not need this self-administered shock treatment. After all, I know I could get a small emergency alarm to wear on my wrist, which would connect me with an emergency center for people living on their own. But self-imposed worries take on a creative life of their own. A new one beckons me: "What if I were to choke on a fish or chicken bone?" Not that this has ever happened to me, but what if it would? I would not even be able to get to a phone in order to notify someone. I suppose that my death would be attributed to fate: That is the way God or fate decreed it. Fortunately this anxiety is not strong enough to make me change my diet to fish fillet or boneless chicken or to turn into a vegetarian.

Then, one day, settling down in my car, ready to start driving, I find myself unable to close my right hand over the clutch or to pull the clutch into gear. All strength has ebbed out of my hand, like a balloon whose air has escaped through an unseen hole. Am I losing my grip on things altogether? Or, horror of horrors, could this be a harbinger of multiple sclerosis? I already see myself as Jacqueline Du Pré, the wonderful young cellist who had to abandon her career as a performing artist when struck down by this dreaded illness. A voice inside me tries to reduce my panic: "Why consider the worst scenario?" it argues, "this could be merely a rheumatic problem." As I repeatedly move my fingers apart and together, my hand slowly regains its strength. Another catastrophe has been averted. Hurrah!

Something was clearly wrong with the lid of the pressure cooker — I just could not open the pressure cooker after having boiled a chicken. Should I call Jonathan in the evening to help me? He was back in town, but terribly busy. No, I thought to myself, I am a big girl now, and where there is a will there is a way. So I waited about fifteen minutes and tried again with all my determination to pry the lid open. Before I knew where I was, it exploded in my face, with the hot contents of the pot and the lid flying all over the kitchen. I felt the left side of my face burning but was more concerned as to whether my glasses had been broken.

Within five minutes I realized that I had been incredibly lucky: My guardian-angel must have taken good care of me. I repeatedly splashed cold water over my face, thereby keeping the pain bearable and decreasing the temperature of the affected area. Nor had my glasses been damaged in any way. In fact, they had probably protected my eyes. Of course the kitchen was a mess. However, it turned out that even my dinner had not been ruined, and a little soap and water cleared the kitchen of my deed.

But my shock had been immense and I shuddered at what might have happened to my face. So I needed to tell the story to somebody for the sake of my sanity. In other words, I needed to abreact. I therefore called Tamara to get the story off my chest and to get a sympathetic reaction from her.

I was delighted that the damage had been kept to the minimum in every way.

In hindsight, perhaps I should have been more dependent and waited until Jonathan could help me in the evening. There is such a fine line between over-dependence and a dependence that is warranted. My judgment is not always the best in this respect.

I must have gone overboard in my wish to be self-reliant and probably projected an image of total independence. I gradually realized that none of my neighbors had invited me, even for a cup of coffee, since Moshe's death. During his last hospitalization one couple did tell me to come up for coffee whenever I felt like it, but I made no use for their kind offer. Another neighbor had put a note through my front-door, inviting me to come up if I wanted to talk or needed any help. Here, too, I had not availed myself of this generous invitation. It became clear to me that they saw me cope and drew their own conclusions. I was not particularly upset about this state of affairs, since we had never been on visiting terms with the neighbors, though we chatted a lot with some of them whenever we encountered them.

Jonathan and Yona, whom I visited in Toronto five months after Moshe's death, spoke openly to me on this matter. They pointed out that I never seemed to need any help or advice, although I was always ready to help and advise others, even when they declared that they could manage on their own.

Thinking about this issue, it became clear to me that I had had to assist Moshe in every possible situation after his prolonged coma, always having to know what was right for him. In fact, I had felt responsible for him like a captain for his ship. I would have to relearn in order to readjust myself. I no longer needed to be both omniscient and omnipotent, able to cope with every crisis. Now I would have to show more neediness myself.

My body taught me a lesson with more long-lasting effect than any argument or persuasion. For years I had not been ill. But one evening, suddenly and out of the blue, I felt dizzy and very nauseous. Would I make it to open the door for Alon, or would I pass out on the way? Alon had come straight from his army reserve duties in order to welcome my London-based sister Rita and her husband David, who were staying with me on a short visit to Jerusalem. I tried to ignore my feelings of sickness, but the feelings would not ignore me. Before I realized what was happening I was vomiting violently. Was it vertigo or had I eaten some contaminated food? As I tried to rest on my sofa, the ceiling seemed in constant motion. How absolutely frightening! But most frightening of all was the thought that I might have been alone when this happened. How would I manage if this "virus" were to occupy my body for a week or even longer? Would I have to ask a friend to move in with me or would I have to move in with my children? After all, I could not even walk to the bathroom without throwing up. So much for my independence. But what human being is totally independent? Don't we all have dependency needs which are strongest at the beginning and toward the end of life, and which are never totally absent? What a fool I had been to believe that I had by and large overcome such needs!

I would just have to relax and enjoy being taken care of whenever the necessity arose in the future. Unfortunately it could not be Moshe, my life's companion for 38 years, who would do the caring and the nurturing, but I realized how lucky I am that I have children who will always be ready in my hour of need.

There are also rewards and pleasures resulting from being alone and unaccountable to anyone, similar to those of living anonymously in a large metropolis. There is a new feeling of freedom and of independence, a comfortable selfishness to single life. And dare I say it? There is even a sense of relief, for, in my particular case, I no longer have to be omnicompetent and solve every problem or crisis that Moshe confronted. Nor do I have to find out whether there are adequate health facilities in the country to which I am traveling. I do not have to ascertain that a certain location is accessible to a handicapped person, and I can run for a taxi after the opera rather than miss all the cabs because of Moshe's slow walking. And I no longer have to leave notes of my whereabouts at home when I go out. The so-called benefits, derived from being alone, lead to confused feelings in me when mingled with the loss and loneliness that I experience.

Martin, who had lost his wife in a car accident, enjoyed the thought that he no longer had to keep order in his house. He also relished the idea of being able to get up late or not at all and of coming home late at night — "too late" no longer existed. He could even break dishes or throw silver spoons into the garbage without anyone taking notice.

How I love to go on walking tours of "Jerusalem Through the Ages"! Moshe was unfortunately unable to join them, since he could not have managed to walk such long distances. Yet he was always angry and upset to be left behind. Not only did he feel he was missing an experience, but it also highlighted the fact of his handicap for him. At times, though not without pangs of regret, I decided to opt out of such tours in order to spare him more mental suffering. I felt this renunciation on my part was not too high a price to pay for Moshe's well-being. Now I no longer have to be so "self-sacrificing."

I do not miss the boredom of the commonplace exchanges that are part and parcel of daily living with another person. Neither do I regret the absence of Moshe's habits which used to annoy me, as when he cleared his throat noisily. I do not even yearn for the drawers which he left open and against which I then knocked my knees or for the disorder in which he left his things. I can burp or pass wind without having to pretend I didn't. In fact, I can forget the basic rules of conduct on which I was raised from early childhood.

No one is present, no one sees me or hears me. And I can do the craziest things now, without having to account to anyone.

The cataract operation which I underwent when Moshe was still alive — the cataract was a result of my strong myopia — left me with one drooping eyelid, so that I looked as if I was half asleep. To cheer me up, my ophthalmologist told me that plastic surgery would remove this esthetic flaw.

I considered undergoing this operation for many months, but Moshe had been adamantly opposed to the idea: "Why go in for elective surgery? Stay clear of hospitals and especially of surgeons!" he pleaded. And who could blame him, after his experience? Also, I knew he had to make sure that I remained absolutely fit and well, since he was utterly dependent on me.

But now Moshe was gone. It followed that I could make my own decisions, regardless of anyone. In fact, I had the luxury of being totally independent. Alon and Jonathan tried to dissuade me: "We love you as you are," they assured me. Or: "Why not have a nose-job at the same time?" they asked, to make the idea of my eyelid surgery sound ridiculous.

Perhaps it was too late now. However, I decided to go ahead and explore the possibility after seeing an enlarged photo of myself. The more my family tried to talk me out of taking this step, the more determined I became to go ahead with it. What was driving me? There was no particular man I was trying to please, as my mother suspected. I knew that the people who liked me, liked me as I was, for qualities unrelated to my looks. But I wanted to look into the mirror and feel good about myself, and thus ready to face another day. I felt compelled to go ahead with this plan, though it entailed having to cancel my patients for two weeks, before I expected to look 'normal' again.

The plastic surgeon gave me the green light. I fixed the date so that I would look alright for Passover — and miss only one week of the university seminar I was attending. There was much swelling and discoloration in the eyelid and the surrounding area for the first few days after surgery, so much so that I was frightened that something had gone drastically wrong during the operation and that I would look a mess ever after. Fortunately, however, the surgery turned out to be a real success story. I had done what I had wanted and needed to do. Hallelujah! The outcome made me feel better about myself and helped to restore my self-esteem.

The dark side of the moon, however, regarding being alone and unaccountable to anyone, is the feeling that no one cares about your behavior and, more importantly, about you, except in a very general sense. You seem to have lost your feeling of belonging and being belonged to. So the wonderful freedom can lead to a dreadful feeling of loneliness and abandonment, with its ultimate expression "Now I can dance all night" turning into "The world is empty and meaningless." Off on your own in a large city abroad, you can call the shots, rejoining your friends and family whenever you want to. But when you are bereaved, there is no such option. You can of course stay close to your family, but only provided you do this in moderation, so as not to lose both your independence and your dignity.

A year after Moshe's death, my territory was overrun by my children. It was I who welcomed them in. I had badly wanted Yona, Jonathan and Tal to stay with me for a short vacation, away from Toronto. What mother or grandmother would have wanted less? Who could have resisted the seductive charm of Tal, who confirmed my statement that she is a real lady by attributing this to the fact that she already her fourth birthday. She now took over my apartment: Though she insisted on sleeping entwined with me in my bed the first night, she cried a lot the next night, with the result that her parents decided to transfer her to their bedroom.

I loved cooking for them and took it for granted that I would do so for Alon and his family, as well as for other close family members, for several meals during the holidays. I now discovered that I had become transformed into a cook, or rather, a restaurateur.

It turned out that the three cousins were having a ball of a time, and in their imaginative play they turned much of the furniture upside down. Moreover my kitchen and frigidaire were eagerly scrutinized for any special treats by three pairs of eyes. Add to this that the two four-year-olds, Neri and Tal, were forever boasting and competing as to who made the better drawings, had more friends and was taller when standing on a chair. Every by-stander was called in for an opinion. Frequently wails could be heard when they quarreled; usually one insulted the other or frightened him or her by calling in a bad ghost.

Meanwhile Yona and Jonathan had spread their belongings over several rooms. The phone was constantly ringing for them and there were frequent visitors who came to see them.

All this came to a climax on the last day of their visit. I was preparing a last supper for them and for at least a dozen other family members, but with the noise and disorder around me, I felt that, as I was performing my household duties, I had become an automaton. More than that, I felt alienated in my own home. In the midst of all this bedlam I tried to take a few last photographs, which would remain as tangible proof of these short but memorable weeks.

To add to all this commotion, Jonathan asked me to go through his father's clothes with him in order to help him choose possible articles for himself. And as if that were not enough, he negotiated on my behalf over the telephone with the salesman of the Macintosh computer company.

The emotional leave-taking and all that preceded it, left me in a state of utter exhaustion. I felt that I had to reappropriate my own home by cleaning and repairing it — even the car's automatic doors had ceased to function, the water was only trickling out of the bathroom taps, and suddenly the main toilet ceased to work. For none of these disorders could I hold my visitors responsible, but it symbolized the end of their visit for me. I spent the following two days partly at work with my patients and partly getting things back into shape.

I reacted somatically, with an upset stomach, to their departure. For security reasons I unlatched the front door and locked it with a key instead, so that it could be opened from the outside. I also called Alon and Tamara to inform them about the steps I had taken. This procedure countered my horror scenario of bolting myself in but becoming too incapacitated to unbolt the door. My windows have iron-bars, so how could anyone reach me to help me, especially in case of emergency when time is of the essence?

It seems that I had regained not only my private space but also my vulnerability, both products of my living on my own; the light and the shadow of this situation.

Now I am back to my splendid isolation, or should I say, privacy? Of course I had ten guests for Sabbath dinner two nights later; though I had wanted to keep it small, Tamara had asked me if I would mind their coming, too. How could I have turned them down?

Have I become too fond of my own space? Does every visitor encroach on my territory? Surely I am not that selfish. In fact, I love having guests. Maybe I have become accustomed to a life which, though filled with lots of content, is largely geared to my own needs. Of course I have to consider the needs of my patients, but their time with me is fixed in advance and is accompanied neither by disorder nor by noise and strife. It is far more controlled. Perhaps that is the secret: I have become used to controlling my own life without, on the whole, having to consider anyone else's needs. When I invite and admit others into my home, I pass on this control, to a large extent, to them. Yet, on balance, my need to have people, especially my children, in my home, because of the joy they bring me, is stronger than the need I have to control my life.

Just before Tal took her leave of me, she prophesied: "Soon you will ask, 'where is my Tiltilon?'" (my pet name for her).

How right she was! I started missing her and her parents as soon as they were gone — noise, mess, madness and all.

Maintaining Memory

Moshe had told me a few weeks before he died that he intended to contribute to the *Festschriften* of two of his colleague-friends, Nahum and Yohanan. When chatting with me, he exulted about the topics he had chosen. But once he left this world, I could not, for the life of me, remember anything about them. This particular memory slate was completely wiped out, leaving no traces. It turned out to be a secret that Moshe took with him into his grave. I felt exceedingly guilty because I could have been the repository of this information, had I only remembered. My failing made me realize that all the events and dialogues which he and I had shared now depended on me alone for their survival. By forgetting them, I was effectively annihilating them and thereby erasing our common past. What a heavy burden to bear! In Milan Kundera's phrase, mine became "the struggle of memory against forgetting."

Unlike Tony Harrison, who wrote, "I believe life ends with death, and that is all," (*Selected Poems*, 1984), I am of the firm opinion that true death does not set in when the heart stops beating and life ceases, but rather when no one any longer carries any memories of the deceased. Nigerians have similar ideas, as I recently learned: They believe that to become an immortal ancestor (that is to say, to live for ever) depends on being remembered by the living.

Shakespeare also did not believe that death sets in when life ceases. In Act V, Scene 1 of *Hamlet*, the Churchyard Scene, the first clown digs out the skull of Yorick, the king's jester, which has lain in the earth for 23 years. Is Yorick dead as a door-nail? Decidedly not, since Hamlet has kept him alive in his memory:

> Alas! Poor Yorick. I knew him, Horatio; a fellow of infinite jest, of most excellent fancy; he hath borne me on his back a thousand times....

Writers and poets have, over the ages made the connection between death and oblivion. Thus *Ecclesiastes* 2:16, over 2000 years ago:

> Of the wise man as of the fool there is no enduring remembrance; seeing that which now is, shall, in the days to come, be entirely forgotten.

More recently, Ronald Dworkin wrote in *Life's Dominion* (1993):

> Death's central horror is oblivion — the terrifying absolute dying of the light.

Suzanne Lipsett, in her autobiographical memoir *Surviving a Writer's Life* (1995), expresses a similar idea:

> The present can so completely obliterate the past, causing those who are buried there to disappear forever.

After his death, I started a search for the lost Moshe, trying to recover any memories I could, both from talking to those who had known him and from the condolence letters I received. I felt that only thus could I achieve a sense of completion and of closure concerning Moshe. But above all, bit by bit, I reviewed his past in memory. Proust might have called this "the gift of recaptured time."

In this remembrance of a life passed, I recalled, lingered over and reflected on all his images, hopes, expectations and regrets.[1]

Oftentime I felt that I am the sole rememberer of many events of Moshe's life — frequently these turned out to be no more than isolated episodes and brief tales — that, in fact, I had become the custodian of his memory or what might be called his 'memory house,' however incomplete its contents. I would now have to remember not only our shared experiences but also all the stories which Moshe told me about his past, particularly about his childhood and his parents. When they died, it was the end of that generation, since all their brothers and sisters perished in the Holocaust.

Moshe was an only child, so that no sibling shared his experiences. Of his own generation there are a few remaining witnesses who, however, shared only very small sections of his life. It is true that he has a cousin who is still alive, but she became psychotic in 1940 when she saw her parents and sister arrested by the Gestapo in a street in Amsterdam. Her family had fled to Holland from Berlin. There is also a second cousin who returned to Berlin after the war, which she spent in Tel Aviv and later in the British army. She was extremely fond of Moshe and nostalgically remembers not only his parents but also his exciting birthday parties when he was a child.

Henry, with whom Moshe went to elementary school in Berlin, was his one remaining friend from those days. He emigrated to Paris with his parents before World War II. We'd meet him on our occasional visits to France or when he came to Jerusalem, but to me it seemed as if we were thereby artificially reviving a former relationship which had long since fossilized.

Of Moshe's past I feel as did Lord Macaulay about China:

---

1. Oliver Sacks, in *A Neurologist's Notebook*, points out: "It is separation in life that we seek to bridge, or reconcile or integrate by recollection." How true also for the permanent separation of death.

> Everything is covered with a veil, through which a
> glimpse of what is within, may occasionally be caught, a
> glimpse just sufficient to set the imagination at work.

Even when Moshe did tell me about former times, I was never quite sure what was fact and what was fiction. After all, we now know that there are two types of truth: historic truth — what actually happened — and narrative truth — a person's account of his remembered experience. Is it not likely, therefore, that Moshe re-invented his life for me — not consciously — in his need to tell his stories so as to make sense of his life?

Had his father Paul (called Paps by Moshe and me) really been so envious of Moshe's school achievements and obvious brilliant promise that he tried to nip his career in the bud? As Moshe related it, Paps took him to a shoemaker when he had completed high school, so that he could become his apprentice. "In Palestine (Israel was created only in 1948 and did not yet exist) you can make a living only as an artisan or manual laborer," he is reputed to have said to Moshe. Had his mother Ilse (called Mams by Moshe and me), who worshipped the ground on which Moshe stood, not intervened and taken him away from there, who knows? Moshe might have become a veritable Hans Sachs, the cobbler. There is no doubt in my mind that he would have been desperately unhappy in this occupation, while the world would have lost a great Semitic and Biblical scholar. (I should add that in later years, when Moshe was a professor, he had no greater admirer than his father).

Both of Moshe's parents were dental surgeons, but Paps gave up practicing his profession when he came to Tel Aviv in 1939. Mams had managed to get him out of the Sachsenhausen concentration camp in which he had been incarcerated during the *Kristallnacht*, on November 9, 1938, when the Nazis burned down the synagogues. He felt that the world owed him a living after what he had suffered in the concentration camp. Though there were two dental chairs in their Tel Aviv apartment-cum-surgery, Moshe's mother effectively took over all the patients, except when someone needed a tooth extracted, when she would call Paps into the surgery to help her. Meanwhile Paps — always impeccably dressed and sporting a diamond ring on the small finger of his left hand — devoted himself to synagogue and community matters, with great verve and a fund of charmingly told anecdotes.

As Moshe grew older, he repeatedly stressed the fact that basically Paps, who purported to be an Orthodox Jew, was nothing of the kind. Moshe even doubted that he fasted on *Yom Kippur*. Mams, who had come from an assimilated Jewish family, kept a kosher household only for the sake of her two men, particularly for Moshe.

The Paps stories as told by Moshe, had some provocative, if not to say outrageous elements. Here was this respected popular citizen, a representative of Jewish Orthodox, middle-class values, who turned out to have a hidden side to him, known only to his wife and son. In it his personal comfort predominated. He lacked ambition and was basically lazy. Even his Jewish observance at home took a back seat when his personal convenience was at stake. He seemed to have two identities, two selves. This was why Moshe was ambivalent toward his father and had little respect for him. In contrast to him, Moshe threw all of himself into whatever he undertook or believed in. Probably his father served as a negative model for him.

Moshe was extremely diligent and exceedingly ambitious, not only for himself but for all those close to him at home and work. Such men are not the easiest to live with, since they pressure themselves and those with whom they come into contact. As far as I was concerned, he insisted that I start to work on my doctorate soon after I arrived in Israel, in order to further my career. There was, however, an additional reason for Moshe's eagerness to involve me in this time-consuming project: He intimated to me that his scholarly labors required that he work late into the night. Hence I would need to be occupied with something that interested me when he was busy. Though Moshe's argumentation made eminent sense to me and I went along with his suggestion, I was not overly happy about it. In those days Moshe felt that time spent away from his desk was time wasted, unless the entertainment to which I wanted him to go was exceptionally good.

Moshe frequently told me how he had had to work in order to support himself during his studies at the Hebrew University; there were no scholarships in those days. He started off as an eighteen-year-old teacher in a school (or was he only seventeen? There is no one to ask about this, unfortunately). His pupils were only a few years younger than he, so that he had to develop the authority and discipline that enabled him to teach the Hebrew and Arabic lessons of the curriculum. This was the cradle for what turned out to be a natural teacher, who was to continue educating students of different ages for more than forty years.

A year before Moshe had his coronary by-pass I was served by a young woman in a drug store. Seeing the signature on my check, she asked if I happened to be related to Prof. Goshen. When she heard that I was his wife, she told me that during the 1973 *Yom Kippur* war, Moshe had volunteered to teach Arabic in her high school — their teacher was serving at the front. She added with great excitement in her voice, how, for the first time in her life, Moshe had imbued her and her class-mates with the thrill and passion of a language to which they had previously reacted with boredom and disinterest.

Like normal Jewish parents — so Moshe told me — Paps and Mams insisted that Moshe have a 'respectable' career, by which they meant a career with a future, in which he would be assured of a decent income. (The shoemaker apprenticeship was no longer mentioned at that point). After all, what was the outlook even for the most brilliant student — and Moshe was doubtless such a one

— who knew more than half a dozen Semitic languages, as well as Latin, Greek and a few Romance languages? There was Prof. Jacob Polotsky, Moshe's teacher, a world-acclaimed authority on Semitic languages and reputedly the greatest, holding down the Chair for Semitic Studies and Egyptology at the only university in Palestine, The Hebrew University. In fact, during the Israeli War of Independence, when The Hebrew University suffered from severe financial problems, there had been those who questioned the need for a professor of an esoteric subject like Egyptology in such an impoverished institution, little realizing that Polotsky, because of his ability to decipher hieroglyphics, possessed the very skills required to decipher codes for the Intelligence service. Nobody expected any other teaching position in the field of Semitics to open up. So, not unreasonably, Moshe's parents believed that he would have to be both sensible and practical, so that he would be able to marry and support a family.

It was therefore decided by the 'family council' that he would attend the three year non-academic law course, set up by the British mandatory administration for the 'natives.' There was no Law Faculty at The Hebrew University in those days. Unbelievable as it may sound, there are still lawyers and judges working in Israel today who received only that legal education.

After two years of Law classes, Moshe decided that he had had enough of Law and therefore discontinued these studies. Little did he realize at the time that within a few years there would be an opening for a young teacher at The Hebrew University. He would have to be the instructor for 'Hebrew Expression' which meant teaching how to write essays. Later he told me, tongue in cheek, that he had never written an essay in his life, but he saw no reason why he should not try his hand at teaching this. Those who appointed him shared his view. They were delighted to provide him with the opportunity to get a foot in the door of the university, the start of his academic career, which was to extend over forty years.

Moshe frequently regaled me with anecdotes about his professors and law teachers, many of whom had been true eccentrics. Fortunately, most of his co-students are still alive, and when they are relaxed at the dinner table, their story-tap can be turned on, and I can again partake of the humorous tales spun around these teachers, most of them long since deceased.

I particularly treasure the story of Moshe sitting in a class where the *Magella* (Turkish law) was taught. Unbeknownst to the lecturer, Moshe had a copy of this law, in Turkish, on his lap and drew up for himself a list of the mistakes made by the teacher.

It has been said by Walter Satterthwait that imagination improves memory and invention amends history. How many recollections had Moshe made up? The temptation to invent must have been very strong, particularly where recollection was hazy. Memories are the stuff of personal mythology; at a distance they are embellished. But as Roland Barthes said: "The stories we tell ourselves about the past, become the past."

Did Moshe revise his or his parents' reality retrospectively? I shall never know. Perhaps he was like Mary McCarthy, who in *Memories of a Catholic Childhood* (1957) turns to the reader, with the following comments:

> There are cases where I am not sure myself whether I am making something up. I think I remember but I am not positive. (p. 9)

and

> I find it almost impossible to sort out the guessed-at and the half-remembered from the undeniably real. (p. 108)

But probably I should not worry on that account since, as Nigel Barley in *The Duke of Puddle Dock* (1991) quipped: "History is not what happened. It is what you remember." In any case, it seems that historic truth, like truth in general, is not absolute but changes with changing circumstances.

Recently I learned that something similar happens within the framework of Roman law: The Romans maintained that from the moment the Court handed down its judgment, the truth became what the Court had ruled.

It was the English psychologist, Sir Frederic Bartlett, who, about seventy years ago stated:

> Remembering.... is an imaginative reconstruction, or construction, built out of the relation of our attitude toward a whole mass of organized past reactions of experiences.

Carol Tavris, in the *New York Times Book Review* of January 3, 1993, has admirably summarized the state of the art concerning memory, which is so pertinent here:

> It (memory) is a process that is constantly being reinvented. A 'memory' consists of fragments of the events, subsequent discussions and readings, other people's recollections and suggestions, and, perhaps most of all, present beliefs about the past.

What Moshe told me about his past, he definitely believed. But it is conceivable that he 'remembered' things which never happened. And he might even have drawn blanks on some of the events he had experienced, though that is more *my* line.

Mary McCarthy considered the fact that she was an orphan as the great handicap to her task of recalling her childhood. She remarked:

> It is our parents, normally, who not only teach us our family history but set us straight on our own childhood recollections, telling us that this cannot have happened the way we think it did and that, on the other hand, did

occur, just as we remember it, in such and such a summer
when So and So was our nurse. (p. 10)

I am an orphan as far as Moshe's childhood and adolescent recollections, as he related them to me, are concerned. But an even weightier issue for me is that there is no one who can validate my own memories of our common, personal experiences, the intimate moments of our togetherness, the details of our first encounters, our courtship, wedding and honeymoon, our marriage with its in-jokes and idiosyncratic forms of language, understood only by the two of us, the birth and raising of our children and our many journeys around the globe.

Worse still, Moshe took with him, into his grave, large parts of my life, the shared experiences which I have either forgotten altogether or can remember only partially and often just dimly. Often I was unable to absorb the numerous new impressions that we shared and would give my right hand to be able to recapture them. Since these experiences were ours exclusively, no one else witnessing them consciously, they cannot be revived, nor can the missing blanks be filled in. Thus, much of the information that was on Moshe's hard disk is lost forever. Fortunately, however, some of it can be retrieved whenever I served as his back-up. Autobiographical elements are inevitably fictional in part, shaped as they are by memory and imagination, by fact and wish, to suit the writer's need to tell a story of the self. Moreover, the passage of time shears away some details and highlights others. Our memories whether good or bad, strive toward a logical sequence. But as in the case of Moshe's recollections, "History is not what happened. It is what you remember."

Déjà vu? Technically speaking, not quite, since there was no television in 1952 when Moshe and I, walking hand in hand through the snow in Newbury, a small English town, where he was teaching at a Hebrew language workshop, heard Queen Elizabeth deliver her annual Christmas broadcast through the open windows of the houses we passed. Now, exactly forty years later, seated in my armchair, I was watching the same queen deliver her Christmas message on television. *Déjà entendu* with no one but myself left to remember that walk through the snow which not only constituted one of my earliest memories of the two of us together, and as such assumed emblematic qualities, but which also turned out to be the beginning of a life-partnership for Moshe and myself.

Who, apart from myself, can remember how, in the summer of 1958, Moshe was called to CineCitta in Rome by the Metro-Goldwyn-Mayer film producers, in order to become their Jewish consultant for the film *Ben Hur*; how, soon after I called him out of a committee meeting at the Hebrew University to tell him about this telegram invitation, he ascertained the facts (to make sure that no one was pulling his leg), arranged for his passport and ticket and flew to Rome the next morning; how, being uncertain about the quality of the film to be produced, he refused to have his name on the rushes, a fact which he regretted ever after; how he bought me a white Gucci leather handbag before his return home, a few days later; how we both flew to Rome, accompanied by twenty-month old Alon, and how we spent four months in Rome in the rented apartment of an Italian Count, situated next to the Villa Borghese, one of the most beautiful parks of Rome; how Moshe and I explored every corner of Rome, including the catacombs, in Moshe's spare time; how he frequently took me along to watch William Wyler direct and Charlton Heston act; how the producer turned to him one day, with the following unanswerable question: "Professor, please do some research in order to find out whether the sheep that grazed on the hills of Nazareth at the time of Jesus were black or white," and how Moshe, without batting an eyelid, had replied "black," whereupon those responsible transported black sheep to the Roman Nazareth film location; how Moshe, after four months of rewriting parts of Christopher Fry's script and directing scenes with Jewish content, landed an offer to stay on in the film world that would have meant moving to Hollywood, in lieu of his academic career in Jerusalem. Last but not least, who but myself can recollect how my mother-in-law earnestly pleaded with Moshe to return to the "safe job" at The Hebrew University rather than opt for work in an industry "going downhill," that would sooner or later close down?

For ever after, CineCitta remained the Paradise Lost in our family saga.

Only I am left to remember Paps's death at the end of Sabbath, during a telephone conversation with three-and-a-half-year-old Alon, while Moshe was at his little boy's side. Alon was enjoying his grandfather's questions to him but suddenly the questions ceased and the telephone receiver fell out of Paps's hand — he had died of cardiac arrest. Of course Alon was oblivious of what had happened, but we, the adult survivors, were shocked by the suddenness of Paps's death, though we also envied him his easy entry into the next world. Little could we have guessed at that time that Moshe was to die of a similar illness, except that no one tried to resuscitate Paps, who was thus probably spared from entering into a deep and perhaps prolonged coma.

My own father was not so fortunate as to die suddenly: He suffered a series of small strokes over more than twenty years. He had become totally dependent on others for all his basic needs and had reacted less and less to those around him. My mother, an unsung heroine, had chosen to look after him at home with the help of visiting nurses. He was finally reduced to a vegetative state and died at age seventy-four.

For Moshe and myself, history seemed to repeat itself, when, just prior to the outbreak of the Six Day War in June 1967, we decided to send our children, then aged eleven and-a-half and seven years, respectively, to my parents in London. We had the gruesome fear that Israel was facing destruction; hence we considered it incumbent upon us to rescue our children. Moshe and I felt, however, that *we* could not, in good conscience, leave the ship.

When we took our leave of the boys three days before the outbreak of the war, we strongly identified with those German Jewish parents who had sent their children to safety in the so-called *Kindertransport*, while they themselves had to stay behind to face death and extinction. It was a most traumatic parting.

Fortunately, for us history did not repeat itself; Moshe and I were reunited with our children a few weeks later.

Who but myself is left to remember our many journeys together, starting with our honeymoon, when we explored the art galleries and churches of Florence, Rome and Naples on foot, with side-trips to Pompeii and to the Isle of Capri, and ending up in Paris? This was the first of many joint trips to European countries.

The last time we returned to Paris was thirty-five years later, when Moshe was already seriously handicapped in his walking. Yet he spent seven hours in the Louvre with me, dividing his time between the Renaissance and Dutch masters, without neglecting the Egyptian treasures. He also insisted that we visit the Impressionist collection at the renovated Gare d'Orsay the following day.

Moshe's omnivorous appetite for knowledge and novelty, as expressed in his unquenchable thirst for art and architecture in Europe and later in the United States — I shall never forget our museum "crawl" in Washington — went hand in hand with Moshe's desire to see Nature's treasures; he had to visit the unique caves as well as the volcanoes in New Zealand and even insisted on flying in a helicopter, which he entered with superhuman efforts, over the fjords of that country. I remember witnessing all this while supporting him with my right arm, as he walked painfully and with great difficulty. But he was indefatigable. Neither could his physical disabilities, however limiting, keep him at home when there were interesting plays or operas presented in London, Stratford or New York.

Only I am left to remember a journey into Moshe's past, a return to Berlin, where he had spent the first thirteen years of his life, forty-five years after he had left it with his parents. Moshe had adamantly refused to return to Germany before that time, but he had received a special invitation from the governing body of Berlin, like other former citizens of that city, and he was willing to try and see if he could now go through with such a journey into his past, to a country which had wrought such havoc on our people.

Moshe complained that since life was good to his family in Germany, it took them almost too long to emigrate; in fact, they decided not to leave Berlin before Moshe's *Bar Mitzvah* in September 1938 — two months before the infamous *Kristallnacht*, in which not only the synagogues were set ablaze, but during which Paps was arrested and interned in Sachsenhausen. They were intent on celebrating the *Bar Mitzvah* in style and in their natural habitat, a society on the edge of extinction. Here they were highly esteemed by their peers, and here they had the financial resources for a real festivity. It turned out to be their last ball on the sinking Titanic and almost cost them their lives. But they did finally leave, just in the nick of time, boarding a luxury liner in Venice, bound for Palestine.

Mams managed to get Paps out of the Sachsenhausen concentration camp by obtaining what was known as a capitalist immigration certificate, a letter of passage to Palestine, good for an entire family. This was no small feat on her part, since such certificates, in spite of their high cost, were almost impossible to obtain.

Of course, their means were greatly reduced in Tel Aviv. Their surgery took over two of the three rooms in their apartment in Ben Yehuda Street, one of Tel Aviv's main thoroughfares. Their problem of building up a new private practice, consisting of patients like themselves, with very restricted means, was not the only one they had to face. Mams found it almost impossible to learn Hebrew. Actually, when Moshe was eight years old, this future Semitic scholar had written a Hebrew grammar for her in Berlin, but she never mastered the Hebrew Language in which verbs are composed of three-letter roots which all sounded identical to her. (When they lived in Tel Aviv, even grocers and greengrocers from Middle Eastern countries had to speak German in order to make a living). On the other hand, Mams was very well versed in German literature, from which she frequently quoted to us. She also had the talent to write comic verse in German for weddings, *Bar Mitzvas* and other festive occasions.

As I watched my in-laws, I realized how important it was for them to preserve their bourgeois standards and pretensions in their new surroundings.

On his return visit to Berlin, it seemed to me as if Moshe had never left that city, since, although it had been very severely bombed during the war, he still found his way around in it easily. The first place to which he meant to take me was the house in which he had grown up. But the house had disappeared, having suffered a direct hit, and so we faced an empty lot. Close by was the former elementary school which he had attended. Now it was used as a school for retarded children. He showed me the tram-stop from which he used to travel to his *Gymnasium* (high-school). The same number was still serving that area. We did not omit to look at the house in which his paternal grandmother had lived. To Moshe's amazement the man in charge of the building was able to show him her name in the book of former residents. We also visited the park in which Moshe used to play, and he pointed out to me the benches on which Jews and dogs had not been allowed to sit.

We attended Friday evening services in Pestalozzistrasse, where one of the only synagogues not burned down by the Nazis in the *Kristallnacht* was functioning again. It was here that Moshe's grandfather had been a synagogue warden, and Moshe was able to point out to me where his seat had been. And of course we went to Weissensee, in what was then part of East Germany, in order to visit the graves of Moshe's and my grandparents (my mother also came from Berlin).

Every residential quarter, every lakeside — such as the Wannsee, at whose shores the infamous conference took place at which the Nazis decided on the Final Solution of the Jews — sparked off childhood memories in Moshe about people who had lived there and of outings spent there on Sunday afternoons. For a short while he had reanimated his past for the two of us, peopling it and suffusing it with life. But alas, it was a world that had vanished. To quote my friend, Shirley Kaufman, the Israeli-American poet:

Like a road in the desert after a flash flood.

Kaufman, 1993

I too felt the need to undertake a similar pilgrimage into my past. When the idea first took hold of me, I could not explain even to myself why I should want to do this, but gradually I realized that I had to complete some unfinished business. After all, I had never really bid farewell to Leipzig, the city in which I was born and in which I had lived for ten years.

In early 1939 my mother, brothers, sister, aunt, paternal grandmother, two cousins and I spent a few months in Engelberg, Switzerland, while my father and uncle, already in London, tried to obtain British visas for us. They were successful, and we joined them just before the outbreak of World War II. I never fully realized then that I was leaving Leipzig for good.

Once before, in 1938, when Chamberlain met Hitler in Munich, my family had left for Switzerland, living in a little town called Baden, but after these leaders signed the so-called non-aggression pact, we returned home to Leipzig.

Now I wanted to see with my adult eyes where I had come from, and to be able actively to take leave of that city which I had left passively half a century earlier.

Unlike Moshe, I remembered very little of my city of origin. Therefore, when I decided on this journey in 1990, soon after East Germany had thrown off its Communist yoke, I asked my friend Marianne, daughter of the former Lord Mayor of Leipzig, Carl Goerdeler, whom I had met years before on one of her annual visits to Israel, to accompany Moshe and myself on this trip.[1]

Leipzig looked drab and dismal; the houses that had been bombed during the war remained as ruins, and the other buildings badly needed a coat of paint. Once this had been a world-renowned commercial and cultural center, with an annual international trade fair, a famous university, the Gewandhaus where the best musicians had performed over hundreds of years, and last but not least, where Johann Sebastian Bach — for 29 years cantor and music director of the Thomas-Kirche — had composed and conducted a new cantata for each Sunday service, as well as the St. Matthew Passion. The latter had been rediscovered a hundred years later by Felix Mendelssohn who founded the Leipzig Music Academy.

I had been led to believe that the house in which I had lived for the first decade of my life, stood waiting for me to visit it fifty years

---

1. Goerdeler had resigned his office when the Nazis took down the Mendelssohn statue; they regarded Felix Mendelssohn as a Jew, though his father had baptized the whole family. Goerdeler helped, in 1944, to organize the unsuccessful attempt to assassinate Hitler, for which he was publicly hanged, while his wife and children were thrown into concentration camps.

later. I desperately wanted to meet the concierge, then take the elevator up to the floor on which we had lived and walk through our spacious apartment, with its elegant dining and drawing-rooms, and the parents' and children's bedrooms.

My most vivid memory of this apartment was that of several of my parents' friends, Jews of German nationality, going into hiding in our home — starting on *Kristallnacht* — in order to prevent their arrest by the Nazis, followed by their probable incarceration in a concentration camp. One of the ways to accommodate so many "house-guests" was to move a few of them, and myself, into the *Fliegenkammer* (literally, fly-chamber) which we proceeded to share with the maid. In this connection I vividly remember looking down onto the street from our dining-room window and seeing our rabbi walking, manacled to two Nazis at his sides. I also still "hear" the banging on the door of our Jewish neighbors upstairs, before the head of the household was arrested.

The members of my family were of Polish nationality, since my father's parents had emigrated to Germany from Poland; although neither of my parents had ever set foot inside Poland; it was almost impossible to acquire German nationality in those days. Due to owning Polish passports, we were not in danger of being arrested at that time. However, several weeks earlier, Jews of Polish nationality had been deported to Poland. But my father was able to avoid this fate by seeking shelter, together with several thousand other Polish Jews, in the garden of the Polish consulate, where Zbigniew Brzezenski's[1] father was consul. As for my mother, she had a gall-bladder attack due to all the excitement and agitation; at that time, medical problems were taken into consideration by the Nazis, who left her to recuperate at home. Nor did they deport children without their parents. So we had all been spared.

---

1. Many years later, Zbigniew Brzezenski was to become Head of the National Security Council in President Carter's administration.

I eagerly looked for the house in which I had grown up in Leipzig, but alas, I was in for serious disappointment: It had been torn down and a new building stood in its place.

After a frantic search I did find the former houses and apartments of my grandmother and various uncles and aunts, though the street names had all been changed during the Communist regime. I girded myself with enough courage to ring the bell of one of these apartments, introduced myself as the niece of the former inhabitants and asked permission to look inside, which was granted. I was told that these large apartments had all been subdivided in order to make room for several families. As I walked through the apartment I could still hear the echoes of my cousins running through the long corridors.

I even went to the adjoining park to which we children had been taken frequently. It still has the beautiful name of *Rosenthal*, which means valley of the roses. While it may have had roses, it never had any sand-boxes, swings or roundabouts. So is it any wonder that I used to hate having to go to this park in which I felt so utterly bored? I cannot for the life of me remember how I passed the hours there. Probably by day-dreaming.

I could not visit our synagogue, the Otto Schill *Strasse* Synagogue, since it had been burnt down during the *Kristallnacht*. To my utter dismay, I absolutely could not find anyone who knew where this large synagogue had once stood.

Years later, on a return visit, when I did find the street, I was faced by a large building plot destined for office buildings. There was not even a memorial stone to commemorate the synagogue.

I was overcome by the sudden realization that not a single person I had known in Leipzig still lived there. They had all either emigrated, died naturally, or been sent to their death.

The saddest part of our visit was to my former school, a Jewish one, which had been turned into a library for the blind. Next to its main entrance, there was a memorial tablet describing the history of this school which had ended up as an assembly place for Jews prior to their deportation to Riga and Auschwitz.

We spent twenty-four hours in Leipzig in 1990. I was glad to see the back of it and had no desire ever to return to this city.[1]

Moshe savored many stories of encounters he had on these journeys to distant lands, especially when they involved cultural clashes. There was the time when the Israeli ambassador to Nepal set up a meeting between Moshe and the Hindu astrologer royal, a highly important member of the king's retinue. This dignitary turned to him and asked: "Is it really true — I find it hard to imagine — that Jews believe in the existence of only one God?"

Years later, when Moshe first visited Germany again, he had an encounter with a bank clerk in Munich (to which we had gone after the visit to Berlin) which he greatly cherished. The clerk, after looking at Moshe's passport, said: "It is strange; you seem to be such a nice person, yet you are our enemy." Moshe who took it for granted that this man related to his Israeli passport and still sported his anti-Semitism openly, was duly shocked. He did not realize that the clerk noticed he was born in Berlin, until he added, "after all, you are a Prussian." So he, as a Bavarian, still considered Prussians to be his enemies, as they had been a hundred years previously.

Another story, which we both treasured greatly, occurred on what turned out to be Moshe's last sabbatical, which we both spent in Cambridge, Massachusetts, in 1987-1988, next to Harvard University. At the time, each of us, independently, used the services of a small printing store which also made Xeroxes. One day, as I collected my Xeroxed manuscript, the salesman, seemingly out of the blue, asked me if I was married. After answering him in the affirmative, I wondered why such information would interest him.

1. Actually I did return to it several years later when I went on an organized tour "In the Footsteps of Johann Sebastian Bach."

"There is a very nice gentleman from abroad, who walks with a stick, living in the neighborhood, and we all thought that you would be so right for each other," he explained.

Moshe and I were both amused and thrilled that, after thirty five years of marriage, even strangers considered us to be a suitable match, just as my aunt in England had done when she heard of our engagement.

One of Moshe's favorite anecdotes about himself concerned an old man who was introduced to him when Moshe was in mid career. The man who had read many of Moshe's books and articles stared at him in disbelief, exclaiming; "Goshen is a living person!" (Goshen *adam chai*). Aware of Moshe's enormous scholarly output and immense reputation, this person could not imagine him to be among the living.

Our memories of people are closely tied to memories of the times and places they have shared with us. After his death, at such times and in those places Moshe was particularly conspicuous by his absence. Thus I realized:

> "It is spring time and Moshe is not there for the *Seder*."
> "It is summer-time and Moshe is not there for vacationing with me."
> "It is autumn and Moshe is not there for *Rosh Hashanah* and *Yom Kippur*."
> "It is Channukah and Moshe is not there to kindle the candles."

Similarly, on my travels, Moshe was missing at my side, starting at the airport, but no less in towns like Los Angeles, Boston, New York, Toronto and London where we had spent much time together. More particularly, when I visited the Toronto Science Museum and saw the wheel chairs, I recalled the time when I wheeled him through this magnificent museum. I remember every ascent and descent in this building, as well as the bathrooms we looked for. At the Toronto art gallery, I suddenly found the cane-cum-seat which I had always wanted for Moshe. I asked the saleswoman to demonstrate it for me and wondered how much it cost. Then I explained to her that I had come upon this object five months too late, since my handicapped husband was no longer alive.

Recently I discovered that my answering machine had captured a dialogue between Moshe and my uncle Werner. Of course we have hundreds of photos and even home videos of Moshe, but to me, his voice and his typical to and fro with my uncle, seemed for a few precious moments to wipe out Moshe's intervening death.

I am particularly pleased that my brother Gershon had taken several black and white photographs of Moshe for my book, *Recalled to Life*, about Moshe's coma and his recovery from it. Gershon is a brilliant amateur photographer and, almost two years prior to Moshe's death, he caught Moshe's typical smile. These photographs are supplemented by some stills I took of Moshe with his little granddaughter Tal on his lap, the two of them looking lovingly into each other's eyes. They stand on my television, so that, in a way, Moshe's presence continually faces me. In fact, when I asked Neri, sixteen months after Moshe's death, whether he still remembered his grandfather, he replied: "No, but I know what he looked like because I see his pictures everywhere."

I don't envisage Moshe as he might have looked one year after I last saw him. As Max Frisch, the Swiss author, said in an interview with movie director Volker Schlondorff, reported in the *New York Times Book Review* of April 5, 1992:

> That is death. A picture that no longer changes. Final, repetition, petrification.

I would add: There is no further aging: He was frozen in time. I will never see Moshe "sans teeth, sans eyes, sans taste, sans everything" (*As You Like It*, II, 7). "Confounding age's cruel knife" (Shakespeare's sonnet no. 63) will never touch him. He was only at the beginning of old age, with hair graying, not white, and he still had all his teeth. He needed glasses only for reading, not for long distance. And, above all, he was still working full-time at two universities. In fact, he had one more year before his retirement. Though he would complain about his imminent retirement, he was looking forward to no longer having to teach and to being able to do research and writing full-time.

In his Last Will and Testament, it is as if Moshe were speaking from beyond the grave. One can hear the typical phraseology, reasoning and argumentation in which he used to engage. It bears the true stamp of authenticity, as a Mozart sonata, Ibsen play, Van Gogh painting or Heine poem bear the imprints of their creators.

Unfortunately Moshe never kept a diary. This might have revealed to us his secret dreams and yearnings, his evaluation of specific events, the occasions that really impressed him and perhaps the ideas he was playing with. With an eye to posterity, he might even have left us his spiritual testament. But this was not the way in which Moshe functioned, and we who survive him are the poorer for it.

Moshe was never motivated to write his own memoirs. God knows that he lived through momentous times: The Third Reich which necessitated his emigration from Germany, World War II, the birth of Israel and several wars imposed on it, the invention of transistor radios, television, plastics, jet planes. Yet he related to none of these events, nor to more personal ones, in writing. Those gifted few who do write their autobiography are assured of a kind of immortality.

Moshe did however leave a collection of letters, most of them to and from colleagues, concerning their work, and quite a number of letters from his parents. Likewise there exists his correspondence with me during the time when we were apart, at the start of our marriage, when I stayed in London to finish my studies in clinical psychology, while he returned to Jerusalem to resume his teaching at the university. These letters constitute a kind of written memory of him during various points of his life.

I was curious to read those letters that concerned Moshe's work, happy to be able to recapture his voice in them and to realize once again what a tremendous impact he had had on his colleagues. But I could not for the life of me bring myself to read his personal letters, especially those he had written to me during our year-long separation. This would have been too painful for me, and I decided to defer it to a time well ahead, which I could not even envisage.

I had to appoint myself as arbiter of which letters were important important enough to be preserved for posterity. I am only too aware of the fact that whenever I destroy a document, it means that I thereby eliminate any record of that event.

Above all, Moshe authored many books and more than a hundred articles. It is these which will no doubt serve as his epitaph as long as the Bible is studied and people take an interest in Hebrew and other Semitic languages. In recent years, several of Moshe's books and articles have appeared posthumously. Has he thereby transcended his own death? Did Schubert prolong his tragically short 31 years of life by having some of his music published and played posthumously?

A very practical question arose, whose implications could have meant relegating deceased members of Moshe's family to oblivion: Did I still have to send money to Weissensee, the Berlin Jewish cemetery, to have the graves of his grandparents, last visited by Moshe and me in 1989, tended? Neither I, nor my children, had ever met these ancestors. There are only very few anecdotes I remember about them. Alon and I decided, arbitrarily perhaps, to continue to maintain the care of only those graves whose inhabitants continued to live in our minds and consciousness long after their death. For us, those were the most significant forebears. The others were truly dead, unremembered and no longer meaningful to us or anyone else we knew.

The beautiful postscript to this decision is that, when I informed the members of the Berlin Jewish community that we would no longer pay for the maintenance of certain graves of Moshe's forebears, they answered that since they had known the Gottstein family well, they would take the responsibility on themselves for tending these graves for at least another two years.

At a social gathering recently, Professor Zeev Falk, one of Moshe's colleagues from the Hebrew University Law Department, described to me a gravestone of a certain Prof. Gottstein which he had seen in Breslau (formerly Germany). How was this man related to Moshe, Prof. Falk wondered. I do not know and will probably never know, although Moshe had mentioned the Breslau professor on a number of occasions. I remembered he had been described as a famous physician, but of what specialty? Again, I do not remember. There is so much information that Moshe took with him into his grave. Does this particular lacuna really matter? Perhaps not, but others do.

> Soon,
> of the two of us, neither will be left
> to forget the other.
>
> Yehuda Amichai, *Love Poems* (p. 100)

I hope that I have chosen the right path by writing about Moshe, so that he will not be forgotten too quickly in an era when no one has the time to remember what happened yesterday.

It is comforting to believe with Vaclav Havel, the Czech president and writer, that

> Our death ends nothing because everything is forever being recorded and evaluated somewhere else, somewhere 'above us.' We are observed 'from above'… everything is visible, nothing is forgotten.
>
> *Summer Meditations*, 1992

Havel calls this "the memory of being" and adds that believers call it God. Surely, for people of faith this is the very nature of immortality.

Anniversaries

There are hotels without the room number 13 or without a designated thirteenth floor because of a superstition that this number is the harbinger of bad fortune. By eliminating number 13, bad luck is believed to be likewise eliminated.

During the first months after Moshe's death, every Saturday night at 12:30 a.m. became an ordeal for me, for was this not the hour at which he had had his cardiac arrest? Since the date of its occurrence fell on the eighth of September, the eighth of every month, likewise, turned into a day of anguish and misery. Six days later, on Saturday, the fourteenth of September at 6.20 a.m., Moshe had passed away. Naturally, therefore, I would wake up around 6 a.m. every Saturday, and the fourteenth of every month became a day of affliction for me. February the fourteenth was the first time that I forgot a monthly anniversary. Had I held on to these red-letter days by force or had they risen out of my unconscious? Who is to tell?

If only we could make anniversary dates disappear as we do the number 13! Imagine calendars, custom-made for each person, in which the death-date of a loved one is missing, as is the date of his or her last hospitalization, the wedding anniversary, the birth-date and for that matter, all the festivals celebrated together in the past. There would be no end to such dates, especially when there are several loved ones who have died. For me, every date would come in twos, since I have two calendars: The Gregorian solar one and

Jewish lunar one. During leap years these may be as much as a month apart.

In this country, the tendency is not to ignore or forget our collective mournful anniversaries. There are three such public ones: The Ninth of Av, a fast day, commemorating the destruction of the first and second Temples. To this has been added Holocaust Day, in memory of the six million Jews who perished during World War II, and the Remembrance Day for Fallen Israeli Soldiers. Public remembrances exert a very high price, especially for Holocaust survivors. Many wounds which have only barely healed, are opened anew annually on Holocaust day, after which a new fragile scar has to grow again.

The idea of being without Moshe on Passover hit me suddenly after reading my sister's letter which contained the line: "How hard this Pessach must be for you this year without Moshe." Tears which I had believed had dried up, now burst out, surprising me. But why was I surprised? Surely such tears are the most expected and natural reaction to family celebrations at which for almost forty years Moshe had not only been present, but over which he had also presided.

My *leitmotif* at that time was 'business as usual.' I tried to keep to the old traditions exactly as in former days. People would ask me:

"Where will you be for the *Seder*? With your son?"

"Oh no," I would answer indignantly, "he and his family will come to my home as before. Let me try to keep things with as few changes as possible."

But since Moshe would no longer lead the *Seder*, he would be conspicuous by his absence. Even the happy faces of my grandsons would not be able to compensate for Moshe's non-existence. I would not be able to kid myself for long; that much I realized.

Nevertheless I tried to put on my best face for 'the general public.' Would I be able to act the smiling hostess, and might the role convince not only the onlookers but even myself, the actress?

Actually, why did I have to act this part and assume that it was demanded of me? Wasn't it an unnatural role under these circumstances? Of course I did not want to spoil the festival for anyone. I felt that my grief was my own affair. But was it really? To say the least, it was shared by Alon and Tamara. I am sure that my mother and uncle were also keenly aware of the missing member at the *Seder*. (Jonathan and his family were in Toronto). Perhaps I was afraid of breaking down altogether, if I were to allow myself any sadness on this occasion. I seemed to see it as an-all-or-nothing predicament in this emotional minefield. For me this was not a time to take small risks, lest they turn into uncontrollably large ones.

I found myself to be weepy in the week before the *Seder*. I hoped that the reservoir of tears would dry up by the time of the *Seder*.

Finally Passover eve arrived. I was not seeing patients that day since it is a public holiday. What a blessing, because I could not have concentrated on anyone else's misery. Or maybe, by helping them, I would have helped myself. They say that distress felt by many is distress halved. But not when the pain is so acute and the thoughts so preoccupying.

I struggled to hold my feelings in check until I could no longer prevent their eruption. Suddenly I felt dragged down by them as I prepared the matzo-balls; as if I'd swum into a calm sea and had encountered a bad undertow. At this point there was no way of stopping my tears. There seemed to be a limitless reservoir containing them. At the end of it, I felt a sense of relief. My family's empathic looks were a solace to me.

I remembered another Passover eve, a time when most Jewish housewives are busy preparing the *Seder*, three years earlier. Moshe was breathing with great difficulty and felt terrible. I finally persuaded him to go to the emergency ward of a nearby hospital, as directed by his cardiologist, whom I had phoned. Since it was a public holiday, only a few doctors were on duty. We waited and waited for one hour, which grew into four, before a junior cardiologist deigned to examine Moshe and ... sent him home.

I also remembered in what bad shape Moshe had been this time a year ago; He was at the tail end of a pneumonia and was so weary and impatient that he became upset when Alon prolonged the *Seder*, as is customary in our family. When dinner was served, Moshe went to bed in order to rest. A couple of days later — it was still Passover — Moshe had to be hospitalized on account of serious congestive heart failure. Jonathan and his family were here from Toronto, and Moshe felt very resentful about not being able to spend fun time with them.

It is our, no, *my* first wedding anniversary alone, without Moshe, today, the 27th of July. Should I regard this date as an aborted 39th anniversary? We were almost becoming freaks in this modern day and age, having been married for so long to each other, and not having changed marriage partners. We would often joke about this.

Tamara called me in the morning and asked: "What does one say?" She did not want to ignore the significance of the day for me. But what does one say, particularly if the day falls exactly eleven months after the death of the marriage partner? The beginning of a new life is rounded off by an anniversary of the death of one's partner. How strange and symbolic! I am pleased that someone remembered it was my anniversary (actually my mother also did so).

Moshe loved to eat out at gourmet restaurants to celebrate such occasions. As chance would have it, I was invited to the wedding of the daughter of good friends today. It seemed appropriate for me to go. I only prayed that I would not start to cry uncontrollably during the ceremony.

Fortunately what I feared did not happen. But the next two days

I felt depressed and cried at the slightest frustration, as when I could not get my typewriter to work. Obviously this was a delayed and displaced reaction. I calmed down as soon as I realized this. Also, talking to Alon about it, made me feel better. He told me that he had felt particularly close to his father the week-end before the wedding anniversary, without knowing why.

It was Alon who wondered if I'd like to spend Sunday evening with him and his family. Since he does not usually invite me days in advance, I asked him for the reason of this invitation. "Its dad's birthday and you may want to be with us" was his reply. How could I have forgotten that date, September 6? It would have been Moshe's 67th birthday, and I had circled the date in my calendar. But my mind was geared to September 8, two days later, when his heart stopped beating and he had to be resuscitated. It was his clinical death, not far removed from his final death either in time or in his ability to function without life-supports. I was surprised at myself. Were the dates connected with Moshe's life less memorable for me than the date of his dying?

Surely I remember him as alive, I thought, especially the events we shared together. However, around September 6 I relived in my mind the last days of his life: The birthday dinner we had with Alon and Tamara at the King David Hotel and the Sabbath dinner the following night, spent at the home of old friends, Shmaryahu and Pnina, where cups were raised to celebrate Moshe's birthday and there was much reminiscing about Shmaryahu's and Moshe's good old student days. On the way home, Moshe stopped every few steps, gasping for breath. The walk, which takes a healthy person fifteen minutes, took us forty-five. As it was Sabbath, Moshe had refused an offered ride.

The problems Moshe had encountered walking home reminded Alon of the events that had preceded Moshe's by-pass operation just over six years earlier. So Alon and I feared a recurrence of Moshe's former cardiac disorder, blocked arteries.

Since that evening was the one preceding *Rosh Hashanah*, Moshe went to synagogue. When he came back he watched *The Glass Menagerie*, by Tennessee Williams, on television. Half-way through, he decided he was too tired to see it to the end. He therefore made himself a cup of tea and retired to bed, soon to be joined by me. Had he continued to watch the Tennessee William play, I would have gone to bed alone and found him the following morning in the living room, dead. As things turned out, however, I was instrumental in having him resuscitated, so that he continued to live, albeit in a deep coma. At least this gave us, the family, a few days in which to become used to the idea of his death. And it enabled Jonathan to still see him 'alive.'

How, if at all, do you celebrate the birthday of a person no longer of this world? We had lived through Moshe's sixtieth birthday several years earlier, while he was still in his first deep coma in hospital. It was like the play *Hamlet* without the Prince of Denmark. Now circumstances were different: His absence was final and irreversible.

I asked myself: "Is there anything to celebrate?" Perhaps the fact that he had lived with us and given us of his best. Obviously the usual Jewish birthday wish "May you live to be 120" was no longer appropriate, nor were the birthday accoutrements, such as the cake with the requisite number of candles or the birthday gifts, called for. Even phone-calls from the four corners of the earth were conspicuous by their absence, except that of my mother who phoned from England to say she had not forgotten.

At Alon and Tamara's home that evening the children realized that we were commemorating Moshe's birthday. Neri came up with an idea: "Let's pretend Sabila is here." As usual, this three-and-a-half year old had responded to the occasion perfectly. By pretending, he had supplied the main, missing person, even if only in fantasy.

That day the question arose for me: Should I visit Moshe's grave? My answer was a clear No. For me it was not his physical remains that determined his presence, but his spirit which was still alive in the home which we had built together and shared for more than thirty years.

The following statement appeared in the Jerusalem Post a short while ago:

> Whenever March approaches, our deep pain starts to be stirred up again.

How well this expressed my own feelings when the first year of Moshe's absence drew to a close. I was what the Germans call "built near the water" (*nah am Wasser gebaut*), that is to say, close to tears, throughout those six days in which Moshe had, a year earlier, according to the Gregorian calendar, been in a deep coma and at death's door. I cried at the drop of a hat, was very vulnerable, easily insulted and, with the help of uncalled for fantasies, felt hurt. And as if out of the blue, I started to doubt all my abilities, including my professional ones.

When the week of the first Jewish anniversary of Moshe's death arrived — a month after the Gregorian date — I had become habituated to grief: I had adjusted to the event so that it provoked a lesser response in me. Also, realizing that I was about to approach an emotional minefield, I trod gingerly; I kept as busy as possible in order to prevent myself from pondering for too long at a stretch. The result was that I was no longer so depressed or upset, in short, so fragile, though I relived every moment of the previous year. My tears appeared to have been staunched up to the day itself. Prepared though I was, I broke into uncontrollable weeping, not when alone, but at the dinner table, in the presence of my children and grandchildren. Later, as I lay down to rest, I hoped that I would have another great dream, as a year earlier, shortly after Moshe had died. But miracles do not happen twice.

We did have a memorial service at the grave-side, where both my sons recited the *kaddish* and each of the family members and friends present read a psalm. I was happy that Moshe has such a beautiful tombstone, with the inscription in specially designed letters. The text, which Alon and I had composed in Hebrew, described Moshe's chief characteristics succinctly, in the order of importance we — and I believe Moshe himself — attributed to them:

A family man
An outstanding teacher
A research pioneer
A renowned scholar

It ended with a verse from the *First Book of Samuel*, 18:14:

He succeeded in all his ways
and the Lord was with him.

We had done for Moshe's tombstone no less than Moshe had done for those many of his deceased relatives and friends for whose gravemarkers he had composed appropriate texts. I was glad we had performed this last service for him and felt that he would have approved of it.

For Violet, even the second anniversary of the death of Malcolm, her husband, was an ordeal. On that day she just had to call Marvin, who had been Malcolm's closest friend:

"I don't know what to do," she wept over the telephone, "shall I kill myself?"

Marvin did not need any time to reflect on his answer: "You should live as rich a life as you can," he advised.

Violet felt a definite sense of relief. Not only had Marvin given her permission to live normally, but since he had been Malcolm's best friend, she felt as if Malcolm himself had granted her this permission. Henceforth she would be able to relinquish the obligation of mourning him. She could carry him inside her heart, cherishing his memory, but without the inconsolable grief that had accompanied her throughout these two years since his death.

The very nature of some anniversaries creates emotional conflicts. Thus, Margaret, a colleague and friend of mine, told me that Sol, her husband, died on the 1st of January, the day of her birthday. For the following three years she could not even contemplate celebrating her birthday, since January 1 had become a day of mourning and remembrance for her. Only as the fourth anniversary of Sol's death approached did Margaret find it in her heart to make the decision to continue to live and enjoy life. She hit on a brilliant solution, whereby she turned the evening of the 31st of December into one of celebration and rejoicing, both for her birthday and for the New Year. The following day, January 1, she set aside as a day of remembrance for her husband. It was then that she visited his grave. She explained that she had been drawn to this resolution of her impasse by a reversal of the way in which the State of Israel celebrates its Day of Independence: It mourns its dead, who enabled Israel to emerge as a country, on the day before Independence Day. Only thereafter do Israeli citizens rejoice fully. I was glad that I did not have to face conflicts of this nature.

Recently I saw in the Jerusalem Post an announcement by a widow twenty years after her husband fell in the line of duty:

Since he was taken from us, every joy has been denied
me.

If this is really true, how dreadful! Why was she unable to complete
her mourning after the usual six to twenty-four months and re-
enter life with its attendant joys and sorrows?

If, however, her statement was not true, why did this widow feel
the need to pretend she was still mourning so intensively after two
decades? Did she think this was expected of her?

Today is the seventh anniversary of Moshe's by-pass operation.
Moshe and I celebrated it the first time around with a dinner party,
attended by Moshe's cardiac surgeon and his wife, as well as by
David and his wife Judy, who had passed that terrible vigil with us in
the hospital waiting-room. During the following years I would
always remind Moshe and my children of that date, but my need to
remember each day following the surgery date in detail grew fainter
as the years proceeded. I expect that this need will, in time,
disappear entirely, and likewise my need to remember the many
other anniversaries connected with Moshe's last illness and death.

It hit me from left field when I least expected it, at the opening of
the International Congress of Jewish Studies, held every four years
in Jerusalem. Moshe had been the section organizer for Hebrew
language and, if my memory does not mislead me, for Bible, at the
previous Congress.

Eight years earlier, he had prepared a major review on the state
of Aramaic studies, which Alon had read in his stead because
Moshe was in a coma. Now, at the opening of the Congress, they
were reading a long list of members who had died during the last
four years. I knew that Moshe would be on the list. But suddenly,
the dam obstructing the flow of my tears, seemed to burst. There

was a flood of tears, and no way in which I could have stopped them. Notwithstanding the awareness that I was surrounded by both friends and strangers, I was unable to hold my anguish at bay. I was so unprepared for this reaction that I was not even equipped with tissues. My loss of control in public embarrassed me greatly and made me feel terrible.

I saw it as symbolic that, exactly one year after Moshe had suffered his cardiac arrest, Prof. Menahem Cohen, one of his star student-disciples, handed me a copy of his scholarly edition of the Jewish medieval commentaries on the biblical books of *Joshua* and *Judges*. Although I realize that he was unaware that he was giving me the book on this anniversary, it meant to me that Prof. Cohen was perpetuating Moshe's tradition.

In the final paragraph of his introduction to this volume he states that it was inspired by Moshe, who unfortunately did not live to see it. Prof. Cohen told me Moshe had said to him that, if he had had the time, he would have wanted to do the research on which this book was based.

> An empty chair, with its empty place at the table, easily becomes an eerie, uncomfortable sight: It insistently calls to mind the person who ought to be sitting there.
>
> Margaret Visser, *the Rituals of Dinner*, 1992

And so it was with Moshe's seat, at the head of the dinner table. Who could sit in it without violating it? It became the symbol of his absence, of his death. Not his television chair, which he loved, but which I would at times grab before he reached it, nor his chair at the kitchen table, where we ate when there was no company. It was at the head of the dinner table that his loss was concretized for my family and me.

This was the very seat on which I had not allowed anyone to sit throughout the five months of Moshe's previous hospitalization. In fact, when Jonathan had seen Moshe's empty chair at the dinner table that first Friday evening six years earlier, when Moshe lay unconscious in the Intensive Coronary Care Unit of Hadassah Hospital, he had burst into tears. Already in those days, the empty chair seemed to symbolize Moshe's absence for him. At that time I did not want anyone to supplant Moshe at the table, though there seemed to be very little likelihood that he would ever be able to come back to it.

Now it was certain that Moshe was gone forever. I would have to face that reality and come to terms with it. By keeping his seat empty, was I pretending that this was merely another temporary absence? Or was there something uncanny about sitting in a dead man's chair? I was unable to answer these questions.

I had never imagined that I'd leave an empty chair for anyone. But now there was not even a conflict in my mind about it. Nor did I wonder whether my friends would consider me crazy for this behavior, which seemed so natural to me. Surely none of them would want to sit where Moshe had been wont to sit.

Whatever the reason, I refrained from letting anyone seat himself in that chair throughout the first year after Moshe's death, except for my Uncle Werner, a regular Sabbath visitor at my home. For it was he who naturally assumed the position of head of the family, and with it he inherited Moshe's seat. But when Uncle Werner was not there, I carefully laid the table so that Moshe's seat remained empty (except on those rare occasions when we had a certain guest who suffered from a severe motor dysfunction, like Parkinsonism, thus needing a lot of space at the table).

Was this a kind of remembrance, the way we remember the prophet Elijah on the *Seder* night of Passover, by filling a cup of wine for him? Surely it was not for fear of offending Moshe, since I do not believe in ghosts. Nor did I think that he is watching from a higher sphere to find out whether he had been superseded, and if so, by whom.

The day arrived when my mother from London joined us at the table and my uncle did not. When I assigned her Moshe's seat, she asked why, and I explained that she was the most senior member of the family at the table. She accepted my reply, and I felt that this problem was about to be resolved.

When Harold, a friend of the family in his seventies, was assigned Moshe's chair by me on a different occasion, he said that he did not like the position at the head of the table. My seat was opposite, at the other end. I claimed that it was I who was sitting at the head, thereby solving Harold's problem.

The problem disappeared whenever we had visitors who had never met Moshe and therefore had no conflicts about occupying his seat. In fact, Boris, a new immigrant from Riga, spontaneously changed his chair because it was too close to the central heating, and moved to Moshe's empty seat.

More than fifteen months after Moshe's death, only Alon and Jonathan are still unwilling to claim Moshe's seat. They would consider it as usurpation were they to sit there. But I have become reconciled to seeing diverse friends in Moshe's seat, though I still plan who it is to be on each occasion.

Reactions of Outsiders

Bereavement is like an open wound. Some cannot bear to look at it or to make any contact with it, for fear of contamination or infection, as if they believed that being in touch with a bereaved family member might cause a death in their own family.

Others want to clean the wound and bind it. They will visit, phone or write, to comfort and support the bereaved. Many will even follow up their contact to find out how the person who has sustained the loss is faring.

Everyone, whether close or not, visits during the week of the *shiva*, some even call occasionally during the following weeks. But thereafter the subject is no longer front-page news. It is not even relegated to the back pages. It is just plainly forgotten until one meets up with the widow by chance. Then, to all appearances, the relationship seems to be unchanged. There may even be some mumbling like "I did not know your new phone-number" or some other feeble excuse. I translated such behavior as "out of sight, out of mind." While each of us thinks that he or she is the center of the world, we turn out to be incidentals for most of those we encounter, footnotes on a page hardly noticed and easily overlooked.

The sad truth will out: Many, though by no means all, of my acquaintances and colleagues, gave no expressions of sympathy to me when Moshe died. They neither visited during the *shiva*, nor wrote or stopped to shake my hand and look into my eyes when they met me. They just ignored me, pretending they had not heard that Moshe had passed away. When I asked, "Do you know that Moshe has died?" I was told: "I was out of the country when it happened." My impulse was to inquire if they had forgotten the art of writing. This unexpressed sarcasm, mingled with a touch of humor, was one of way of fending off my deep hurt and anger.

The psychoanalyst who touched me lightly on the shoulder with her forefinger and called out: "I am sorry" as she dashed off, upset me deeply. Was this all the sympathy she was capable of mustering? In my eyes these non- or minimal reactors failed the test of simply being human. Without this basic quality how could they be therapists? After all, it is not an attribute one can switch on and off in different situations.

My immediate feeling of outrage was soon replaced by a sense of bewilderment and even curiosity: Why had so many of my colleagues in the mental health area, who had to deal professionally with human problems and painful situations like bereavement on a daily basis, shown themselves so deficient in their reactions to my loss? Did they invest so much energy and empathy in their patients that they thereby exhausted their resources, thus making them unavailable for use outside their clinic?, I wondered.

When I discussed this question with an American psychoanalyst friend, he suggested a different explanation: Since these colleagues had become accustomed to distancing themselves from their patients and to not expressing their own personal feeling to them — all this for professional reasons — they carried this behavior into their non-professional lives, where it was most inappropriate and came across as non-caring.

While this explanation made sense to me, it did not enable me to forgive them.

A week after Moshe died, I met a distinguished colleague of mine in the street. He had just been informed about Moshe's death. As if to balance the scales, he told me that his mother had recently passed away.

"How old was she?" I inquired.

"Ninety-two years" was his reply.

I really did not feel the two events were comparable. In fact I resented his attempt to equate them. Are a mother's and a husband's death in any way similar, especially if the mother, in a far away country, has reached a ripe old age, while Moshe was only sixty-six years old at the time of his death? It boils down to the fact that very few emotional events are similar in any but the most superficial ways. He who tries to equate them, rather than providing comfort, merely causes anger in the other person.

I felt that the response from another colleague, who enveloped my hand in hers and said: "I don't know what to say," was far more appropriate.

I was intrigued by several bright, sensitive women, colleagues of Moshe, who hugged me with a lot of feeling, and said spontaneously that they must visit me, but then never made the slightest attempt to do so. Was the idea of being alone with me in my bereavement too threatening for them? I would just have to accept their intention for the deed.

I also collected a number of promised dinner invitations which, however, never materialized, since the persons who intimated that such invitations were in the works, failed to come through with them. I did not encounter this phenomenon when Moshe was alive. When push came to shove, was I considered to be too unimportant to be regarded as a possible dinner-guest? Or did my potential hosts fear that I would spoil the atmosphere by reminding everyone of Moshe's death, thereby bringing their own mortality a little closer?

The bottom line was that I had learned on my own person what I had known theoretically for a long time: That the way many people react to death is by avoiding the person who remains behind. This is a fact of life I just had to accept, like the weather, realizing that there was nothing I could do about either of them. I tried, nevertheless, to carry on a relationship with the people involved.

I do not believe that I ever behaved in this avoidant manner toward people who had lost a close relative. But this may be due to the fact that I am a psychologist and know how important contact is, especially after a major loss. But the man in the street is probably unaware of this. Also, I realize that people vary widely in the extent to which they can share the distress of others. While some can tolerate a high degree of involvement in the misery of their friends and colleagues, the rest will tend to avoid any potential source of anxiety. They do not seem to have the ability to invest energy and devotion in the pain of others.

So I lost some friends but gained others. Inexplicably there were those who spoke of the need to keep up contact with me after the *shiva* but did nothing about it. Whenever I took the initiative — I am not too proud to do so — and tried to invite them, they were busy but would make at most one attempt to call or ask me over. Implicitly, they did not consider me worth cultivating once Moshe, the great Professor, was gone. Yet I am sure that most of these people continued to see themselves as good friends of mine and were totally unaware of their behavior and the feelings it aroused in me. I know that I could always depend on their attendance at memorial meetings, but did they really think that was sufficient? Probably they did not think about it at all. Only I did the thinking and discovered that I had become marginal for part of my former social network. It took me about a year to realize that there was nothing I could do to remedy the situation.

It is said that many wives are afraid that their husbands may start up with a single woman, whether divorced or widowed, which is why they refrain from inviting them. I am quite convinced that this was not the case among these friends. Rather, it was a lack of attention among people with very busy professional and social lives. They just did not take the time and imagination to consider what it means to lose a marriage-partner, to be left on one's own. Perhaps it is impossible to identify with a widow until one stands in her shoes — I have certainly learned a lot from my own bereavement. But maybe these friends just dared not allow themselves such empathy. After all, how many people are able to come face to face with a negative situation which could one day be their own?

Unfulfilled promises, in the nature of "We must see you soon," are excusable, perhaps, in very busy people. But are they sensitive to the needs of widowed friends? Should not words mean something and intentions be translated into actions? Maybe, due to my psychological training, I am more aware of the importance of keeping up close, more intensive contacts with bereaved friends, first and foremost on the telephone. Once-a-year-get-togethers are too meager a fare for good friends who have sustained a major loss. *Façons de parler* that may be appropriate under normal circumstances have to be adapted to the widow's new situation, which requires tact, empathy, warmth and an ability to listen.

For a long time I ruminated over the question how not to feel too hurt about losing certain friends, following on the loss of my husband. Then, one day, the answer came to me in a flash: "Stop having expectations about how people should behave to you, so as to prevent being disappointed by them."

I suppose it is natural that we expect certain behaviors from people we like and to whom we feel close: A showing of interest and concern, a readiness to be close. But all these gifts, beautiful when bestowed, are not necessarily available. Without expecting such gifts, the pleasure of receiving them is doubly great. And above all, when they are not forthcoming, the disappointment is only minor.

It was before Jewish festivals like Passover that some friends, who had not contacted me for months, remembered to call and wish me a happy holiday. Rina, with whom I have never been very close, said she had thought about phoning me a hundred times but never got down to it. I suppose that, like many others, she trembled at the idea of having to talk to a widow. What if she were to break down during such a conversation? Or if she had to confront what it means to be a widow, an idea she probably wanted to push as far out of her consciousness as possible. Who knows, by talking about it, one could even make it operative, God forbid. The result of all this internal and barely suppressed anguish was for her to defer the act of telephoning until her husband or her conscience could no longer tolerate this deferment, that is to say, until the eve of a Jewish festival. I hope that my way of seeing the situation was not based on wild assumptions.

Shelly, a friend and colleague who lost her husband Jack about a year after Moshe died, told me about one of her acquaintances, who confided in her that she was careful not to mention Jack's name in her presence. Her reasoning was that she thereby hoped to spare Shelly any further feeling of grief. Shelly explained to her that her mourning proceeded, irrespective of whether other people did or did not mention Jack's name. Hearing this, the acquaintance expressed a sense of relief — she could now talk naturally to Shelly, without any self-imposed restrictions.

This episode made me wonder how many other taboos people impose on themselves vis-à-vis widows, thereby making the actual meetings with them extremely burdensome for themselves and, therefore, if at all possible, to be avoided.

Fortunately there were numerous good friends who called, invited, visited, and showed they cared in many different ways. One woman friend would send me magazine cuttings which, she believed, would interest me. There were couples who invited not only me but also my uncle, whom I tended to host over the weekends, for Sabbath and festival meals. One friend offered to accompany me to hospital for a small surgical procedure, and others asked me to join them when they went to the cinema, though this was a rare occurrence. I knew I could call on these and others whenever I felt the need to do so.

One of my great fears was to become an object of pity. In order to avoid this I tried not to compare myself unfavorably to others when in company. Thus, when the table talk centered on vacations spent together as a couple on a cruise, for instance, I did not intrude a jarring note, by exclaiming: "Alas, this is the type of pleasure which I can no longer contemplate, since I am alone." The one exception, I remember, occurred when the conversation centered on sabbaticals. Then I could not but exclaim the fact that this would have been Moshe's last sabbatical which we were about to spend in Philadelphia, at the Annenberg Center.

Perhaps, not surprisingly, it was the widows who lost their husbands about a year before or after me, who were most interested to keep up close contact with me. We were, of course, kindred spirits who had much to share, even if we were each quite different personalities, with different life-histories. But there was an openness in each of us to hear and to listen. I enjoyed meeting them on a one-to-one basis but not in groups, where the distinguishing feature that we all shared was that we had each sustained a major loss.

Nora, a widowed friend, shared with me her consternation at having been invited by her late husband's former colleague and his wife, together with four other widows. She was convinced that they meant well when they planned such an evening, but Nora was not amused; neither was she pleased about it. She felt that she had been classified according to one characteristic only: The fact that she had lost her husband. The meeting put salt on her wounds by accentuating not only her loss, but also her new status within her social circle.

Phyllis, the widow of a well-known professor, felt humiliated to be seated at the widows' table, at the back of the hall, at social functions of her late husband's college. To her it symbolized her social demotion. As it is, "widowhood means a plunge in social status in our society, which still places a woman's value on her relationships with men." (Helena Lopata, Sociologist).

I am an accordion. There were days when I eagerly sought out people, especially single women. I met them for lunch or went to the movies with them or just chatted to them on the phone, which enabled me to stay at home but to feel connected. On other days I preferred to immerse myself in reading, which I passionately love to do in my free time, rather than in cultivating more and more social relationships. At those times, I felt that since my work connects me with people a good portion of the day, and since I set aside part of the week-end to meet with my family and friends, my social needs were adequately covered. Yet I could not help but wonder: Is this a chickening out of a challenge too great for me, the challenge to invest in social relations and even to acquire new friends?

The joy of visitors from abroad who stayed with me, even if only for a few days! The warmth and affection of these friends, and their enabling me to share in lives and worlds outside my own, have become even more important for me, a person who lives on her own, than for couples or families. And the delight I experience in the knowledge that, come what may, their friendship and love will always be mine! As Frank, a friend and colleague of Moshe's from Harvard, expressed it: "Old friends are the best friends." It is pleasurable to look after them and to make them feel welcome by providing for them on a daily basis, after being used to providing for only myself.

I started to see patients as soon as the family from Toronto left Jerusalem. Up to that point I had been surrounded by my closest family. Now, I felt, it was time to get on with my usual occupation. Work provided me with a good opportunity to concentrate on the problems of my patients rather than on my own. It also prevented me from sitting at home and feeling sorry for myself. I am firmly convinced that self-pity is the worst feeling in which to indulge, since it does not lead anywhere except to further despondency and depression.

All my patients were aware of Moshe's death because it had been publicized in the newspapers, on the radio, and on television. In some parts of Jerusalem there were even street-posters announcing his death. (When Moshe was hospitalized I asked Tamara to phone my patients and tell them that I could not see them at present, due to my husband's severe illness).

Two of my patients phoned and asked if they could visit me in my home after the *shiva* was over. They had been abroad when Moshe died and were extremely upset to hear my news. I saw them, separately of course, and appreciated their making the effort to commiserate with me. I realized it could not have been an easy step for them to take.

Some patients later reported having had difficulties in trying to figure out how to relate to me under these circumstances. Sherry said that she had considered calling me but, not knowing what to say, she had desisted. After all, it would have meant a change of roles. Anna told me that she almost did not return to therapy because she did not know what to say and found this very troubling. I helped them to express what Moshe's death had aroused in them. A number of patients were then able to express their fear that I might die and leave them just as Moshe had left me. Yet most patients, after mumbling something about being sorry, went on to talk about their own problems. This is, after all, the reason why they came to see me in the first place, not in order to hear about my troubles. Anything else would have constituted a reversal of our usual roles.

One day Lionel came to his session and recounted the awful night and day he had spent in the hospital, where he had had to take his mother. He told me in great detail about the upsetting events he had had to face there, many of which were familiar to me. Although he had insisted on knowing the details of Moshe's last illness and hospitalization, he was totally oblivious of the feelings his story might arouse and how it would resonate in me. At first, this surprised me. But thinking it over, I understood that he was in a state of shock. His experiences were of recent origin and he just had to talk about them.

Letters from friends meant a lot to me, especially those condolence letters which brought home to me the different aspects of Moshe, treasured by those who had known him, and how much he had meant to each of them.

Ernest, a medical friend from Yale, wrote:

> We grieve with you for Moshe. To have known him will always be one of the highlights of my own life.

Moshe also got rave reviews from former students like Daniel:

> I have treasured being a student and junior colleague of Moshe's for many years. He was instrumental in encouraging me to come and live and work in Israel. Not only did he have one of the best minds of his scholarly generation in Jerusalem and one of the most erudite but he also had great scholarly and personal integrity.

Moshe's loyalty to his students also was far beyond the norm.

Jules, a medical friend from Boston, wrote a very personal appraisal of Moshe:

Moshe was an extraordinary person and knowing him was truly a privilege.... Most of all I will cherish his memory for being an individual with whom I could have fun. He had a great sense of humor — a blend of the scholar's intellect and the little boy's joy in the foibles and paradoxes of daily life. He would vent expressions of these inner delights in the form of charming-multilingual quips, which were simultaneously insightful and entertaining.

Frank wrote one of his rare letters a few weeks after Moshe's death:

We mourn our loss of Moshe, an old and cherished friend (and an admired colleague). There are only a precious few such friendships, and we grieve as they fade away. Moshe was a very great scholar, but I think of him also as a man capable of firm and long-term friendships (when he was not called upon to give a critical and scholarly judgment).

It was important to me to answer each such letter, since I knew the writers had taken pains to pen them. Whenever I was able to keep up a correspondence, I continued to feel in touch with these friends and to sense that they were participating in my life, even if at long distance. I enjoy letter-writing, but even more do I enjoy receiving letters into which people pour themselves. I am fortunate in having several friends whose letters I really treasure. In this day and age, when most people use the telephone rather than having recourse to pen and paper, I count myself lucky in this respect.

Out of the Mouth of Babes

When I was growing up, two topics were never mentioned in my family: Sex and death. We lived in London from the beginning of World War II, where my father was the president of the local Jewish Burial Society, but he could not tolerate the mention of death in his home. A ruling had been introduced into his Burial Society, forbidding women to attend funerals of even their closest family members, since the men did not want to see them weep and wail. They would not have known how to deal with distressed, sobbing females and would have found them too disturbing to watch.

I remember, years after I was married, the children, Moshe and I passed through London at the end of Moshe's sabbatical year in Boston, on our way back to Jerusalem. It happened to be the first year after my father-in-law's death. We had mentioned this to Alon, then five years old. As the whole family sat over their breakfast, Alon recalled that it was George Washington Day. Excitedly he exclaimed: "Then saba (grandpa) and George Washington can have breakfast together up there." Moshe and I smiled at each other, but my father hushed up Alon. I got the impression that he felt that talking about the deceased was dangerous and could lead to further deaths.

We now know that children fortunate enough to have reassuring, comforting parents and grandparents are themselves likely to remain calm, rather than anxious and fearful, when faced with the death of a close family member. Naturally, we tried to behave in accordance with this principle when Moshe died. Therefore we were determined to allow my grandchildren to talk freely about this event; in fact, we encouraged them to do so, in order to discover their fantasies and to prevent possible fears, guilt feelings and conflicts from arising out of this issue.

My young grandchildren were of particular significance to me at the time of my bereavement. Not only did they serve to divert me but, more importantly, I saw them as extensions of Moshe (and of myself, of course). Thus, I could think of Moshe as continuing to live in these adorable little kids. They had his intelligence and charm and, here and there, I even saw a physical resemblance with him in certain of their features.

Their relationship to his death held me in fascination, since it was naive and unadulterated — they meant what they said and had no ulterior motives for their statements, which is not always true for their elders.

For all three children, death was "going up to God and/or to Heaven." This is obviously due to what they had been told by their parents.

All three children referred to Moshe as "sabila." Why did they adopt this curious name when the Hebrew word for grandfather is "saba"?

The etymology of "sabila" goes back one generation to the time when Alon was a toddler. He would address his father by the Hebrew word "aba." But whenever he called "aba, aba" and Moshe did not appear at once, Alon added variations on the name: "abale" and finally "abila." It was "abila" that stuck and came to be used by the mother's helper we employed, as well as by Moshe's closest assistants. It even appears on the "pillow" of Moshe's gravestone.

From "abila" the step to "sabila," a combination of "saba" and "abila," was very short. This therefore was the way Moshe came to be affectionately called by my children and grandchildren.

Tal, who was three years old at the time, witnessed her parents, Jonathan and Yona, break down and cry when they were informed of Moshe's likely death while they lived in Toronto. She became very sad, not only because she saw her parents in this unusual state but also because she had very fond memories of her "sabila."

Tal arrived with her mother in Jerusalem three days after the funeral. It was she who informed me: "Your man is *met* (dead)." Demonstrating a truly feminine concern, she asked me: "Who will make *kiddush* (the benediction over the wine on Sabbath) for you?" This little girl turned out to be more far-sighted than her grandmother, who had not yet worried about that issue. At her tender age, she was showing a concern for and sensitivity to my needs, which deeply touched me and which constituted the beginnings of what Carol Gilligan in her book *In a Different Voice*, called: "The Female Ethic of Care." When I visited Tal and her parents in Canada later, she refused to go to Day Care because she did not want me to "be alone."

Neri is four months younger than Tal. When I went to see Moshe in hospital, I asked this little boy whether he knew why I was going there. His association with hospitals, where his mother works as a birth enabler, was clear from his question to me: "Do you want a baby?"

When Moshe died, Elisha then six-and-a-half years old, worried aloud: "If my mummy or daddy die, can I become a man?"

In his mind he had transported death to the next generation, to people whose death would most affect him. He had doubts whether he could develop into maturity without the assistance of one of his parents.

Not only was Elisha anxious, but he was also sad. He expressed his sadness in a picture he drew of a Ninja turtle against a totally black background. When I asked him: "Why black?" he said it was because he had found a black crayon. Needless to say, he had every other color crayon in the same box.

Neri's first reaction to Moshe's death was a kind of denial:

"I can get sabila back," he announced. "Ill bring a large ladder and climb up on it."

"What will you do when you reach the top?" I wondered.

"Tell him to come down," he answered, as if it were the most natural thing in the world.

By the time he was three years old, Neri added a postscript to his ladder suggestion: "He is dead and won't come back."

On another occasion he announced: "If you go up, you can't come down again. Sabila is dead."

Though from time to time he still asked his parents when his grandfather would come down, the fact that he had been faced with Moshe's absence for three months must have brought the finality of his death closer to him. It is hard for adults to accept the finality of death — how much more so for young children.

Meanwhile, Tal and her parents had returned to Toronto, where she repeatedly asked them about every person in Jerusalem whom she knew, whether they were dead or not, "especially Bentzi," her fourteen-year-old uncle, who was her favorite and whom she wanted to marry when she was grown up. Since one person close to her had died, how could she be sure that others would not do so as well? Her basic stability had been put in jeopardy.

The first Passover without Moshe took place half a year after his death. Neri, then three-and-a-quarter years old, turned to me with: "You have no family now. Sabila used to be your family but now he is..."

He glanced upwards. "How did he get up?"

Elisha explained: "His body is buried but his soul, which is like wind, rises up to God."

Neri then looked at Moshe's photograph, facing him on the kitchen window-sill, and informed me:

"Now I am your family because sabila is not your family any

more. He is with God. If I would go up to God, there wouldn't be any Neri. I don't want to go up to God."

The subject had become too close and frightening to him, since he had allowed himself to identify with sabila.

Elisha turned to Neri: "If you put a rubber-band around your neck, you'll die. Do you know what happens then?"

Neri retorted like a shot: "I'll be with sabila."

A few weeks later, after he had absorbed the idea of the body and soul being separated after death, Neri suggested: "Sabila could come down and put on his body again."

So the soul was the vital part of a person, while the body was like a garment that could be put on or taken off, as required. He seemed to be a native Buddhist....

I visited Jonathan, Yona and Tal when Tal was three-and-a-half years old. In her play she said that she was "a little dead," which reminded me of the young woman who declared that she was "a little pregnant." Tal invited me to talk to sabila on her toy-phone.

When I asked her whether I should call her father "daddy" or Jonathan, she answered: "Daddy — sabila died, so you don't have a daddy. Jonathan is your new daddy."

For her, not only were the concepts of father and husband identical (as is usual at that age), but in her mind her father could easily become my father too. She assumed a kind of adoption of me by him, though she was aware of the fact that Jonathan is my son. How easily people can substitute for one another at that age! But the main point is that she generously offered to share her beloved daddy with me, a fact which moved me deeply.

Having been told that her grandfather had died due to illness, it was hardly surprising that when Yona took to bed with a flu while I was there, Tal's first question was whether her mummy would die.

At Day Care there was talk about grandparents with her friends.

She declared that she has two sabas (grandfathers) and two savtas (grandmothers). When someone questioned this, she admitted that one saba was dead. However, he had obviously remained on the list — gone and yet present.

She informed me one day: "Part of your family is dead. Why did he die?"

I told her that sabila had been very sick. She had her own explanation for that: "Because he smoked."

Living in Canada and watching a lot of television, she must have heard of the connection between smoking and serious illness. Incidentally, Moshe was a non-smoker.

Tal returned to the subject five months later, on my next visit to Toronto. Again she asked: "Why did sabila die?"

Again I repeated that he had been very sick. This time she replied: "So he goes up. There, he'll get a check-up because he was sick."

It was clear that, as far as she was concerned, the rules and behaviors of life continued "up there": Whoever is sick gets a check-up.

A few months later she declared: "He died. He's up in the sky with God. They made him go up in a special angel that could fly. When you fly, you get to be with God."

She was then just over four years old and the technical question of her grandfather's transportation upward clearly preoccupied her. She hit on a solution that seemed to satisfy her.

Nine months later, when I visited the family in Canada again, Tal informed me: "Saba (grandpa) Yossi and Savta (grandma) Miriam (Yona's parents) and you are all young grandparents. When sabila died he was a very old man."

Since at this stage she admitted that she no longer remembered Moshe, she was able to reassure herself about death: Only very old people die and those around her, whom she loves, are all young. So death had lost its sting for her.

A few days later she told me: "I miss sabila terribly but you miss him even more."

I was really touched by this little girl's insight that Moshe's death affected me more than it did her. But realizing that she no longer remembered him, I was intrigued to know why she would miss him at all.

Her explanation for this was: "He didn't know me when I became big."

She was obviously aware of the changes she had undergone since her encounters with Moshe and that she was no longer the tiny tot he had known. Her statement reflected pride in her growth and development which she wished her grandfather could have shared.

Four months later, when the Torontonians had returned to Jerusalem, I asked Tal whether she remembered anything about sabila. She straight away answered that he had gray hair and a big smile on his face. Who is to say whether she really remembered these details or whether she deduced them from Moshe's photos?

Soon thereafter she added: "I am lucky you didn't die."

But her sad afterthought was: "But your husband did."

With real concern Tal inquired how I had managed *Yom Kippur* by myself, without them in the house (they lived with me for a week when they came back from Toronto but went away for *Yom Kippur*). I assured her that I managed quite well on my own.

Looking into my eyes, she said: "But it is nicer when we are here, right?" She was always full of empathy, even at her tender age.

Two weeks later, this little girl showed her concern about relationships in a typically feminine way:

"Sabila died," she started, "so you could get married to somebody else. He'd be my daddy's daddy. What will he be for me?" She answered her own question after a moment's thought: "Saba (grandfather). As an afterthought she added: "But he has to be really old because you are old."

(Four-and-a-half months earlier she had told me that I was a young grandparent, unlike sabila who "was a very old man" when he died).

"Then" [when you remarry], she continued, "you could have a girl — so far, you could only have boys, like Lonny (Alon) and daddy, and my mummy and daddy can only have girls."

In her eyes I am a candidate for remarriage; matrimony is the natural state for adults to be in. Moreover, people are replaceable: Sabila died — someone else can take his place. Her father and she would thereby acquire a new father and grandfather.

As far as she is concerned, age doesn't enter as a limiting factor in regard to having children. With my remarriage, the gender balance in my family would be restored at last. Three birds would be caught with one stone.

Twelve months later, when she was already six years old, Tal asked me if she could lie on sabila's bed with her shoes on. To my "No," she responded:

"Because we still know him, so we care about him, right?"

By "still knowing him" she probably meant "remembering" him. She implied that as long as we remember him, we have to consider his wishes — in this particular case, not to have anyone lie with his or her shoes on his bed. I was amazed that for Tal as for me, remembering the deceased is the crucial factor.

She added: "My mummy and daddy could have more kids but *you* can't because you don't have sabila."

She no longer thought of my replacing him with another husband, for the sake of having more children, including daughters.

About a month later, she asked me how old sabila was when he died. When told he was sixty-six she reassured herself that age had not been the crucial factor in his death, by explaining to herself and me. "He was very very sick. He had a million viruses. Was his illness catching?"

Whenever anyone in her close family became ill, the reason

given was "a virus," which made the bearers highly infectious. So this was the most likely kind of illness for her grandfather to have had. But all these former patients are still alive in spite of having had "a virus." Hence she concluded that sabila must have had a "million viruses." That is to say, the quantity of viruses determined his death.

Yet, she empathized with me by adding: "Its hard for you that he died."

She did relate to the age factor, both in those she loved and in herself. She wondered how old I am and guessed an age well below sixty-six years, which to her probably meant that I was not yet old enough to die. She followed this with the direct *cri de coeur*: "I don't want you to die." And then, as if to cheer herself up, she said: "I have another hundred or sixty years to live."

The reason for Moshe's death also perplexed Neri, who asked me about it. I explained to him that Moshe's heart did not work very well. Neri's reaction was:

"When *your* heart won't work too well, *you'll* also die and go up. And when *my* heart won't work too well, *I'll* die and go up and meet you there."

His anticipation of a grand reunion in Heaven held his fear and sadness at bay. Life, as far as he was concerned, continues above in the same way as below. Also, what happened to sabila could be applied universally, as far as Neri was concerned — first to me, then to him, and presumably to everyone else: Just as everyone eats, drinks and sleeps, so everyone's heart will fail one day and they will die.

When this little fellow was four years old, the grandfather of a boy in his nursery school was run over and fatality injured. Neri said to me:

"My mummy told me that Uri's saba died. Your husband died (this was the first time he made the connection that his grandfather was my husband). I thought, where was he when I came to you and he already died?"

The death of Uri's grandfather reminded him of his first realization, fifteen months earlier, that <u>his</u> grandfather had died. He had never previously told anyone that he had wondered at the time where sabila was.

Eighteen months after Moshe's death, Neri, who was staying with me for Sabbath, was cuddling with me in my bed. He looked at the bed next to mine and said:

"Chester (the dog) is sitting on sabila's bed, but he (sabila) doesn't know it because he's in the sky (Neri did not know the word heaven)."

At this stage there seemed to be a clear separation in his mind between what is here, on earth, and what is above, "in the sky." The two were no longer connected, as far as he was concerned. Gone were the fantasies of bringing his sabila down.

Eight months later I wondered if Neri remembered anything about sabila. It was almost two years since Moshe's death. Neri suggested that I ask him questions, which is a sensible way to retrieve memories.

"Where did sabila sit in this room, usually?" I started. Neri pointed to the easy-chair by the television.

"Which was his seat at the table?" I continued.

"At the head of it, where Uncle Werner now sits," he replied.

He was right in both instances. When I asked whether there was anything else he remembered about sabila, he demonstrated Moshe's slow walk. Moshe did walk slowly after he recovered from his coma, but Neri gave a different explanation for this: "He was very old." It was clear that this little boy thereby defended himself against the fear of dying. He inquired how old his grandfather had been when he died. The answer made him anxious, since he realized that I was close to that age. I therefore reassured him that sabila had died because he had been very ill and not because he was so old. I continued that I did not think I would die at the same age as sabila had done and added that his other grandfather was quite a few years older but still alive. This had the desired effect on Neri, calming him down.

Of course I am sad that these young children can only dimly remember Moshe and will soon forget him altogether. I feel that they have lost a grandfather who could have given them so much and could, in turn, have been delighted by them.

Reintegrating into Daily Life[1]

> Events, challenges and life transitions do not just
> happen to people. People respond to them, and cope
> with them, in different ways, so that it is necessary to
> focus on the process of *negotiation* of life experiences
> and not just on their impact.
>
> *Michael and Marjorie Rutter, 1992 (p. 8)*

People make short term allowances for those who have sustained a loss, but there comes a time when they expect you to return to 'business as usual.' That does not mean that you can dispense with your feelings of bereavement, of sadness, of solitude, but you would be well advised to try and take up activities unrelated to these. Such activities have a momentum of their own. If you are able to become interested in them and to enjoy them, they take you a step away from your grief, even if only for a couple of hours a day.[2]

To make sure that you will not be forgotten in your own life-time, it is important that you maximize your assets, that you look your best, that you are interesting and fun to be with, that you are a good hostess, and above all, that you are someone who cares for

---

1. Weiss (1988) speaks of 'recovery' when there is a return to ordinary levels of effective personal and social functioning. This requires freedom from pain and distress and the ability to experience gratification.
2. As Sally Friedman (1996) points out: "It is up to each individual to choose his or her solace." (p. 182) "There is no one way, no tried and true system." (p. 183)

others. It is easy to become obsessed with your own worries or daily preoccupations, thereby limiting your horizon to your own doorstep. But who wants to be in the company of such a person for any length of time?

The ideal medicine is a challenge: Taking up a skill which you dropped earlier in life or starting to learn it anew. What a great self-confidence builder! This could entail any of a host of disciplines, such as basket weaving, painting, writing, playing a musical instrument, photography, or studying for a diploma or degree. It could also consist of volunteering in a home for the aged or in a hospital, guiding in museums, helping new immigrants to settle or assisting children with learning difficulties. If you are able to apply yourself to any such undertaking, your mind cannot at the same time preoccupy itself with your own misery. Apart from this, it will give you a new purpose in life, something for which to get up in the morning.

I have tried to acquire skills which I did not need before. Thus, I took driving lessons again after I had dropped driving for ten years. Even after Moshe's prolonged coma, he was miraculously able to drive again, and I was happy to be his passenger, although I had the vague fear that something might happen to him at the steering-wheel. But I put my trust in God.

I was determined to learn to drive again, however long it would take me to do so. Deep inside me I questioned what need I had to drive the car, which belonged to me alone after Moshe's death. Weren't there enough buses and taxis in Jerusalem to transport me? But it was a challenge I had imposed on myself, and Shlomo, my teacher, was convinced that I would ultimately become a good and safe driver. My old driving license was still valid, since I had renewed it annually. This meant that I would not be required to pass another test. Hence all I would need was driving experience.

Finally the great day arrived when Shlomo felt that it was safe to let me drive on my own. I did not even feel anxious, though left to my own devices.

Yet the temptation to take the easy way out and not to venture forth on new challenges were numerous:

"Why shouldn't I take a taxi rather then drive a way with which I am unfamiliar?" asked the tempting voice.

Moreover, Alon felt that driving was just not for me.

"Shlomo enjoys not only your sense of humor but also the extra income he derives from you," he said. "It's nice to have a life-long pupil."

But I believed that Alon was somewhat biased in his opinion since he and Tamara could always make good use of my car. Yet, as if to support him, a hundred excuses reared their ugly heads in my mind, trying to lure me into not treading hitherto untrodden paths: "I will get involved in an accident, I will lose my way, there will be no parking-space in which I can park."

But counter-arguments lined up against these: "Here is the great opportunity to prove myself; driving my own car will enable me to get away quickly; I can never learn new ways unless I actually try them out."

And besides, I had to prove Alon wrong: I would not be anybody's life-long pupil. I felt ten feet tall whenever I opted for the harder way and learned, in the process, that I am still able to grow. Above all, I came to love driving and the new-found freedom it bestowed on me.

For years I had avoided contact with a word processor. Since, in a test I had taken decades earlier, my mechanical ability had been evaluated as equal to zero, I felt certain that I would never master the skills of handling a computer. However, Jonathan with all the persuasive powers he could muster, finally convinced me that, if I was writing another book, it would be utterly foolish for me not to acquire a Macintosh. A few weeks after I bought this word processor, and with a couple of lessons behind me, I actually enjoyed my new toy and was proud that I had overcome my resistance to it. It was a triumph of will power.

But my heart grieved for Moshe, who had adamantly refused to consider such an instrument, especially after his coma, since he had lost his manual dexterity in the left hand, so that typing had become problematic for him.

For forty years he had worked on a modern Hebrew dictionary as large in scope as the Oxford dictionary. But since each word was written manually on a card, only the first letter "aleph" was close to completion at the time of his death. It is clear that not many people would buy a one-letter dictionary, even if this Hebrew letter happened to contain all five vowels. Had Moshe, however, agreed to computerize the dictionary and his other research institutes, this scholar, who had accomplished the work of at least five men in his lifetime, would have managed immeasurably more, as Jonathan, an inveterate user of computers, made clear to me. But Moshe, like many of his contemporaries, had been adamant in his refusal to modernize his undertakings. Instinctively, he must have felt the task of learning this new technology to be beyond his grasp.

Though I celebrated the enormous output of his work, I was also saddened by what he left unachieved. How much time he could have saved and how many projects he might have completed, had he overcome this fear and prejudice by both of which he had been obsessed.

There is a sense of achievement in being able to acquire new friends in my own right, and not merely because I am the wife of Moshe. Sheba, to whom I was introduced at a friend's dinner, wanted me to be what she called the "center-piece" of an evening she arranged.

What could have been more flattering to me? Actually, she tied in marginally with my life with Moshe, since the first thing she told me, when we met, was that she had heard so much about my book whose subject is Moshe.

The first time I entertained people whom Moshe did not know, I wondered whether this is what is known as 'starting your own life.' Of course Moshe was mentioned, since the Cohens were from Oxford and the talk veered naturally around Moshe's post-doctoral year, spent mainly at the Bodleian library in that divine city. There was also a couple whom I had met on a guided tour of the Dead Sea area. Saul had recently published a book about his work with cancer patients, which naturally brought the talk to my book about Moshe. All roads lead to Rome….

Being an older woman is problematic in Western society. It is hard, if not impossible for her to find romantic love and fulfillment on account of her age. Yet it cannot be appropriate for her to wallow in the trough of self-pity.[1]

At times I was overcome with a yearning to be treated as a woman again — not merely as a psychologist or hostess or mother or grandmother, but as a person with a specific gender who evokes gallantry in a man, giving her the feeling that he is interested in her figure and features, as well as in her head and heart.

Gradually such men started to make their appearance again on my horizon. One of these, whom I still knew from the States, as he had been married to a friend of mine who later died of leukemia, intimated his physical inclination for me. However, I was not in the least attracted to him since I shared no interests with him: He was a business man, valuing only material goods and creature comforts.

---

1. Through the advent of the Internet in the 1990's, it has become much easier to find new friends, and possibly lovers — perhaps even husbands.

Fortunately my body and my mind work in tandem — I cannot and do not want to separate them.

Slowly I began to notice that, whenever I was around men, the sense of mortality was present. Those men I encountered, who were a little older than myself, were confounded by the encroachments of age; invariably they mentioned their diverse health concerns, investigations and treatments, from glaucoma check ups to colonoscopies, hip replacements and coronary by-pass surgery, as well as their fears of memory loss and Alzheimer's disease. None of these are really conducive to a romantic atmosphere....

Unfortunately, those men I did find attractive and who exhibited a similar inclination for me, were unavailable for a host of reasons, the chief being that they were married or of a different faith. They tended to be brilliant, charismatic, warm, well-read and witty, but also narcissistic, totally absorbed by their work, and mostly unconcerned about the reactions they evoke in others. The inevitable disappointers. But at least I could enjoy their scintillating talk and let my fancy roam. And who needs such men on a long term basis anyway? Later perhaps, I will opt for a different kind of man: The reliable, considerate and less narcissistic kind. Meanwhile I sleep diagonally in my bed. In other words, I remain alone.

Talking about disappointments, it was inevitable that there were occasions when I looked forward to an evening to be spent in the company of a good friend. However, sometimes, at the last minute, he became ill, or had to attend an urgent meeting or had to hospitalize his mother. However reasonable the excuse, I was upset and disappointed. I could have spent the rest of the day weeping and feeling sorry for myself, when the anticipated pleasure had been so great. But after allowing myself a few tears of frustration, I would decide to go to some event which I knew I would enjoy; it could be a concert, a lecture or a film. Through such compensation I would divert my thoughts and feelings, to some extent at least, and prevent my descent into depression.

I think I am fortunate to have had an unusual husband at my side for almost four decades and to have borne and raised children who are loving and affectionate. I am also lucky because, in spite of having grown up in a middle-class Jewish Orthodox environment in London, where it was unheard of in my youth for a woman to go to college, I was able to do so. There my eyes were opened and my imagination was stimulated. I have never since stopped thinking, reflecting and, above all, dreaming. In short, I know that I have inner resources to make something out of my new existence. I refuse to allow the tragic feminine myth "I am nothing without my husband (or boy-friend)" to govern the rest of my life.

What is true on the mental level applies no less to the physical one. If you don't use your limbs for a while, you become stiff. Whether you walk or swim or cycle, horse-ride or jog, you keep fit and feel well, at least as far as your body is concerned.

I, whose only exercise used to be jumping to conclusions, until I had to accompany Moshe to the pool, continued to go swimming about once a week. I also joined exercise-classes to prevent osteoporosis, to which all post-menopausal women are prone and which can lead to broken bones, especially hips, at a later stage of life.

From the time of Moshe's cardiac arrest I would not allow sleepless-ness, from which I then suffered, to become a problem. And above all, I never talked about how I had slept, since I find the topic as tedious as talking about one's health or the weather. What gives anyone the right to start his or her day by boring their fellow-men in this way?

Rather than worry about being unable to sleep and how this might affect me the next morning, I would either read or watch television. I decided that, if I felt unduly tired the following day, I would take time off, even if only for a short while, in order to rest and make up for some of my lost sleep.

Immediately after Moshe's death, I would wake up between five and six o'clock in the morning, although I went to bed after midnight. My sleep was prolonged to 6.30 a.m. only three months later.

On the other hand, when life practically came to a standstill in Jerusalem on account of the snow, I felt sorely tempted to stay in bed and perhaps not to get up at all. To confound matters, I felt overwhelmingly tired in the evenings, long before my usual bed-time. But I believed I had to overcome the siren-call of my bed by interesting reading-material, appealing television programs, or by making phone calls. In hindsight, I think I should have given in to the urge to stay in bed for a day or two at least, until I had been freed from my inordinate tiredness. Maybe I was too harsh on myself.

But I was a firm believer in self-control. I made myself get up at a set time in the morning, forced myself to dress properly and to eat within limits. Like Bernard Shaw, I can resist anything but temptation, which is why I avoided buying such foods as French bread or cheese cake. Above all, I kept up a routine of sorts, even if not a rigid one, by seeing patients and reading and writing at fixed times.

However, my routine was balanced by spontaneity. I always left myself open to the unexpected, whether in the form of an unforeseen invitation or of an unplanned encounter. My motto became: "Seize the moment."

Nothing is easier than to have amorphous time at your disposal which you can waste by daydreaming for hours or by making endless phone-calls, reading innumerable newspapers, or watching television for hours. The last of these alternatives enforces passivity and exerts what George Kennan calls "a peculiarly drug-like, almost narcotic, soporific power over people."

Time, like water, condenses, evaporates into thin air, and before you realize it, there is none left. You ask yourself: "Where has my day gone?" but are unable to provide an answer. It has disappeared, and there is no outstanding feature that might enable you to recall it. The amorphous mass, has, like a cloud, moved away, without leaving you anything to which you can hold on, even in your memory. Days and weeks can pass in this way and your life passes away with it, without new impressions being taken in. This is the very hallmark of barrenness and sterility. It was clearly what I most feared might happen to me, causing me to become such a harsh task-master to myself and to impose a routine on my daily life.

Buddhism teaches that suffering is caused not by reality, but by our attitude to reality. This is demonstrated by the different ways in which people react to pain, illness and other upsetting circumstances.

I was reminded of this idea when I stopped my car at a red traffic light, too close to another car — in fact, my right-hand mirror scratched the left front of the car of an elderly woman, who ran out of her car in order to shout at me and to write down my name and that of my insurance agent. She could not understand, she said, how I could have been so idiotic as to cause this damage. I tried to staunch the flow of her accusations by apologizing, but to no avail.

Later, as I continued driving, I wondered whether I would ever have become upset in the same intense way if someone had left a small scratch on my car. I just could not work myself up, even in fantasy, since too many other weighty issues were preying on mind: There was a close friend, ill with cancer, who preoccupied me, and I was anxious about another friend, suffering from acute panic attacks. As long as the damage was merely material, I thought, and nobody had been hurt, why work yourself up to a frenzy? Surely everything is relative.

Recently, Donald, an English friend of mine, wrote to me from London that he had complained to his analyst that his wife was crazy, and reportedly received the following reaction from him: "There are worse things in life than having a crazy wife." Donald could hardly believe what he heard, since his wife also happened to be the mother of his children. It took him a long time to figure out what could be worse, until he came up with the idea of 'losing a child.' This realization brought home to him the fact that even extreme suffering is relative, depending on one's attitude to it.

I try hard to keep everything in proportion and not to let minor incidents unrail me. One may well ask: How do I define 'minor'? After all, one man's minor is another man's major. When you consider people worse off than yourself, most things become minor.

It was neither the sea-side nor the mountain air which I craved for my vacation. What I cherished above all was meeting old friends, especially those who had known me when I was a half of one whole couple. Would they be able to appreciate me now? Since they knew my past, I felt that they had a more rounded picture of me, one with greater depth.

My trip to Boston in the summer of 1992, where I had many friends, showed me that I was not merely Moshe's widow but also a person liked for her own sake. Sarah wanted to spend as much time with me as I had available. Caroline took a day off work to be with me. Millicent, a curator in one of the largest Bostonian museums, showed me around the Nubian exhibit, and June and Marvin not only hosted me in regal fashion in their beautiful home throughout my stay, but June also prepared a dinner fit for kings, to which she asked many of my friends. I was invited out by other friends for innumerable meals to homes and restaurants, and on each occasion I was chauffeured around in true VIP fashion.

A similar story was repeated in New York, with a different set of friends.

I realized that I could no longer go abroad during my vacations, without joining a group of other travelers. Moshe and I had always carefully prepared ourselves for seeing those countries we were about to visit, with the help of travel guides, and, whenever possible, had consulted friends who had been there. In this way we were able to indulge our own special interests: Visit as many churches and temples and go to as many museums and art galleries as we pleased, and for as long as we liked.

Now this way of traveling was no longer an option for me. I would just have to pick the group which would arrange the trip closest to my heart. Of course I could never know beforehand how such a group would be constituted, how high a threshold the majority would have for taking in places of cultural interest, rather than for going on shopping expeditions. It was potluck, for instance, when I decided to go to China and Thailand this way. Moshe and I could not have gone there on our own either, in view of the fact that neither of us knew a word of Chinese or Thai. I just hoped for the best.

The primary shock came when I realized that, as in Noah's ark, people went everywhere in pairs! The tables were laid for even numbers. So where was I to sit? Again my nose was rubbed in the fact that I was solitary, at night, when my fellow-travelers retired to their bedrooms, two-by-two, while I went to my single room. It evoked a longing in me, a yearning for the man with whom I could chew over the day's event and in whose arms I could fall asleep.

The constant togetherness with the members of the tour group was not easy for me, particularly since most of them did not share my interests or *Weltanschauung*. Yet I found it more difficult than heretofore to be on my own when I returned home. Apparently I had got used to being around people for most of the day and was missing this element now.

Twenty months after Moshe's death I had the following dream:

> I precede Moshe upstairs to our apartment and, as usual, automatically bolt the front-door after having entered. When I hear him come up, I hasten to the door to unbolt it, Moshe tries to open the door with his key and becomes impatient when he does not succeed. But I know that the door will be opened soon.
>
> I am happy in my dream to be dreaming this.

Moshe follows me upstairs as he was wont to do, since he was the one who parked the car; also he was motorically slower than I, after his long coma. But I seem to have forgotten that he is coming behind me, since I automatically bolt the door, thereby excluding him. I no longer expect him to follow me and have become self sufficient, having rebuilt my life without him. When I do realize that he is there, I try to let him in, that is to say, back into my life. He is impatient, as he used to be when something did not immediately work the way he wanted it to.

There is a technical problem about letting him in: Our actions are uncoordinated. But is this only a technical problem? His key cannot open a bolted door. In other words, he is no longer able to open what was our common front door, due to my action on the other side.

I am reminded of Orpheus and Euridice, though there is a change of gender. I am Orpheus, leading Euridice-Moshe who is so near and yet so far. The good intentions to readmit him are there on my part, and he obviously wants to come back, though an obstruction on my side makes his reentry impossible now. But the content of the dream makes me happy, and there is a feeling that the desired outcome of our being together is about to happen any moment. Having completed my mourning and restructured my life, of which Moshe is no longer part and parcel, I look forward to his rejoining me, but on a different level than heretofore, even though there are obstacles on the way to achieving this.[1] Yet there is an air of optimism in the dream that this may be possible very soon.

Three months thereafter, on what would have been our fortieth wedding anniversary, I dreamt the following:

> I am staying in a rented vacation home. There is a ring at the door. It takes me a while to open. I expect Moshe to come up — he is living below. I open the door with a big welcome-call for him, but it is a family with fair-haired children who enter.

To start with, I was baffled by the content and meaning of this dream. In order to understand it I first of all tried to remember the events of the previous day. It was a day I spent in Bangkok where I had been with Moshe and our sons twenty-five years earlier. There I bought myself a ring with small sapphires, driven by an inexplicable urge to do so. The realization came to me suddenly: This is what Moshe would have done — he would have taken me to a jewelry store and asked me to choose something I really like, to celebrate this anniversary. I was now doing what my internalized Moshe wanted me to do: I was spoiling myself. Throughout my China-Thailand trip I was acutely aware that it was Moshe who had

---

1. Silverman and Klass in *Continuing Bonds* (1996) state: "People are changed by the experience (bereavement): They do not get over it, and part of the change is a transformed but continuing relationship with the deceased." (p. 19). "The resolution of grief involves continuing bonds that survivors maintain with the deceased and these continuing bonds can be a healthy part of the survivors' ongoing life" (p. 22).

SURVIVING WIDOWHOOD

provided the means that enabled me to undertake this fantastic journey.

That evening I was reminded of Moshe in many diverse ways: The hotel at which we stayed the night of the anniversary was similar architecturally to one in which Moshe and I stayed in Fiji in 1988. Also, we were only two days away from returning home via Amsterdam, where Moshe and I had rented an apartment for a few weeks many years previously. Last but not least, several people in the tour group mentioned the fact that it was the fifteenth of Av (a Jewish month), a popular day for Jewish marriages (after the close of the three-week mourning period for the destruction of the Temple). I told them that this had been my wedding date.

In the dream I live above, while Moshe lives below — in the world of the living and of the dead respectively, but as in my last dream, I expect him to come to me in the vacation-home, as he did in the one we rented in Amsterdam. When all is said and done, isn't it natural to be together on vacation and to celebrate a wedding anniversary together, especially a fortieth anniversary?

The ring at the door is, in all likelihood, connected with the ring I bought myself the previous day. Why does it take me a while to open the door? I probably want to prepare myself mentally for Moshe's visit. After all, it would not be an every-day occurrence to have such a visitor.

But Moshe no longer appears; nor does he any longer have a key to let himself in, as in the last dream. He really is in another world, 'below.' It is this reality that I have to accept.

The people at the door are young. They represent a new generation, one unknown to me. It is these people whom I have to allow entry into my life now. They are fair-haired, that is to say 'different' from me. The future is different and, though the welcome greetings I extend are meant for Moshe, these new, young and different people are the ones who receive them.

"Does your husband live in Jerusalem?" I was asked some time ago at a social gathering.

"Yes, he is buried in Jerusalem," I answered without thinking. For the rest of the evening I tried to puzzle out why I had given such an odd reply. It certainly had the effect of preventing further questions about how and why Moshe had died. The incident occurred just under two years after his death, when I felt that being involved in probing by an absolute stranger about this topic, was no longer appropriate.

But I wanted to explore the meaning of my reply on a deeper, less conscious level, since it was clear to me that it had not been filtered through my thought processes. It was important that I had equated living and being buried. Moshe's last remains were now "domiciled" — another word for "living" — in Jerusalem. But over and above this fact, as far as I was concerned, he was still living in our minds and memories; his spirit was alive, especially in Jerusalem, the city in which he had resided and worked.

Pockets of vulnerability remain. My tears of sadness may suddenly start flowing freely at the time of Jewish festivals, when the experiences I shared with Moshe on such occasions well up before my mind's eye. It is then that I realize that our common past can never be fully recaptured, even by the best of memories.

Or, there are times when loneliness overwhelms me. Perhaps it is an existential loneliness, since living is a very lonely thing. Whatever its cause, my loneliness can be assuaged only by someone who is close to me. At those times, there can be no substitute for a man I love. It is a feeling that makes me restless and unable to concentrate on anything else. Life seems pointless and inane, a veritable wasteland. All I can do then is to crawl into my bed and pull the blanket over my head. Perhaps a good cry will calm me down. And then to sleep. After all, in the words of Scarlett, the heroine of *Gone With the Wind*: "Tomorrow is another day."

When all is said and done, Patricia Weenolsen, in her book *Transcendence of Loss over the Life Span* (1988), gets right to the crux of the problem when she says:

> We can never completely 'get over' a major loss in the sense that all its effects are negated, that it is 'forgotten.' Our losses become part of who we are, as precious to us as other aspects of ourselves, and so does the transcendence of those losses. (p. 57)

Andre Dubus, in *Broken Vessels* (1992) speaks of the physical pain of grief becoming "a permanent wound in the soul." How could it fail to be so when one considers that, according to an American study, the loss of a spouse is the most traumatic event in a person's life?

The American feminist, Germaine Greer, in *Women, Aging and Menopause* (1993), praises midlife:

> Autumn can be long, golden, milder and warmer than summer and is the most productive season of the year.

I consider myself as still facing autumn, with winter a good way off. Perhaps this is a self-delusion, but I do believe that it is not chronological age which determines life. The decisive factor is how old one feels and acts.

When my grandparents were in their fifties, so I am told, they would dress in black and behave like very old people, moving very little and demanding the respect of those approaching the end of life. Nowadays, not only is the life expectancy much longer, but people in their fifties are usually at the zenith of their lives, successful and recognized in their professions and reaping the fruits of their labors. They can be not only in good health but also still physically attractive. At this stage they are able to enjoy those pastimes which they could not afford earlier because they were too busy raising a family or too strapped for money. Now is the time to rejoice in the abundance of life. Even in their sixties many of them carry on with their work and hobbies and... play on the floor with their grandchildren.

I have a high regard for Betty Friedan's conception of old age as a new life stage in which further growth can occur, with new strengths and possibilities emerging.

Henry James said:

> The way to affirm one's self... is to strike as many notes,
> deep, full and rapid, as one can.

What a marvelous motto for life!

There are moments which I cherish and which make life worth living. Not merely when one of my grandchildren runs into my open arms with a big smile, or when a patient tells me how I have changed her life, or when a couple informs me that they will stay together as a result of the treatment, but also when Sandra, a friend, calls me from New York to tell me that she has used me as a role model, having decided for the first time since her husband's death two years earlier, to invite all those people to a dinner party who had invited her during the intervening years. She feels that I have enabled her to make a breakthrough. No longer does she have to feel indebted to people, being merely on the receiving end of their hospitality, but she has now become a giver, someone able to reciprocate. I treasure equally Shari, a new friend, who says that the best thing at the festive dinner we both attended recently was meeting me and adds: "I feel you are part of our family now." Several young women friends have adopted me as their mother-confidante. This role gives me great pleasure; I am particularly happy when they express to me how much this relationship means to them.

The common thread in all these special moments is the human element, when I make a positive difference to someone, who appreciates this and reciprocates with warmth and affection: When it means that a connection between two people has been established, it has the power to banish, at least temporarily, the feeling of aloneness, which is the widow's lot.

Time does not resurrect the dead, but, as the well-known proverb has it: "Time is a great healer." In my own particular case, two years after Moshe's death, the searing pain caused by his passing disappeared for me and with it, the inevitable tears. On the occasions of Moshe's birthday and of the anniversary of his death, I no longer feel the need to mourn or to live every moment preceding his cardiac arrest and last hospitalization. Of course Moshe is constantly on my mind at those times, but awareness of his absence no longer causes me suffering. Tranquility has supplanted poignant emotions. In short: I have made my peace with Moshe's death. The words of the Jewish funeral service, befitting my new acceptance of what fate decreed for me, ring in my ears:

> The Lord has given, the Lord has taken, blessed be the
> name of the Lord.

Other widows may reach this acceptance earlier or later than I did. One can only hope that reach it they ultimately will.

Twenty-six months after Moshe's death, I have the following dream:

> I walk in the street with Moshe, wondering how this is
> possible since he is dead. But I very much feel him as I

walk arm in arm with him and he explains something to me which I think no one but he could know or explain to me.

In the next scene he and I become involved in a very passionate sexual encounter.

The 'old' Moshe, as he was in his best days, has finally re-emerged, the one to whom I looked up admiringly and who engaged and satisfied not only my mind but also my body. At long last, the Moshe to whom I was attracted and who was my lover in every sense, surfaces. The handicapped, dependent Moshe had displaced him in my memory until now. But, having completed my mourning, I am open to reconnect with the whole, undamaged, active man whom I married. It is someone who is irreplaceable ("something which I think no one but he could know or explain to me"). He is very much alive and physically present in my mind now.

> I will be more sane if I have been able to accept, to include, to harmonize more and more of my experiences.
>
> *Touching the Rock*, p. 123

Thus wrote John M. Hull (1991) at the end of his account on becoming blind and on the frustrations of blindness.

How well I can transfer his statement to my experiences of widowhood: Like Hull, I, too, could not have written a stoical or matter-of-fact book. Like him I did not try to continue life as if nothing had happened after Moshe's death. Like him I needed to probe the experience and to grapple with it. To see it as part of my life and to understand its particular characteristics, never forgetting that widowhood is only one aspect — albeit a very major one — of my life, among many others, just as blindness is for Hull.

It seems that what the American historian Natalie Zemon Davis terms 'stubborn vitality' drives human beings to try and make and remake their own lives, no matter how severe the constraints placed on them.

Above all, I have tried to show that, as in the case of Hull, *at* (or *after*) the most despairing point, there comes a change: No longer an agonized sense of loss and of mourning, but instead the realization that it is possible to prevail over adversity. This is accompanied by a new sense of life and identity.

In the final instance, life's losses define us, chipping away at the rough surface until we become who we are. Widowhood then turns into a metaphor for resilience.

Bibliography

Amichai, Yehuda, *Love Poems*, Schocken, 1986.

Barley, Nigel, *The Duke of Puddle Dock*, Viking, 1991.

Bartlett, Frederic C., *Remembering*, Cambridge University Press, 1932.

Brener, Anne, *Mourning and Mitzvah*, Jewish Lights, 1993.

Brothers, Joyce, *Widowed*, Simon and Schuster, 1990.

Caine, Lynn, *Widow*, William Morrow and Co., 1974.

Cole, Diane, *After Great Pain a New Life Emerges*, Summit, 1992.

Diamant, Anita, *How to Comfort the Dying, Bury the Dead and Mourn as a Jew*, Schocken, 1998.

Dubus, Andre, *Broken Vessels*, Godline, 1992.

Dworkin, Ronald, *Life's Dominion*, Knopf, 1993.

Ebaugh, Helen R. F., *Becoming an Ex*, Chicago University Press, 1988.

Ericsson, Stephanie, *Companion Through the Darkness: Inner Dialogues on Grief*, Harper Perennial Library, 1993.

Felber, Marta, *Finding Your Way After Your Spouse Dies*, Ave Maria Press, 2000.

Friedman, Sally, *Swimming the Channel: A Memoir of Love*, Henry Holt, 1996.

Gilligan, Carol, *In a Different Voice*, Harvard University Press, 1982.

Gorer, G., *Death, Grief and Mourning in Contemporary Britain*, Tavistock, 1965.

Goshen-Gottstein, Esther, *Recalled to Life: The Story of a Coma*, Yale University Press, 1990.

Greer, Germaine, *Women, Aging and Menopause*, Fawcett, 1993.

Harper Neeld, Elizabeth, *Seven Choices: Taking the Steps to New Life After Losing Someone You Love*, Counterpoint Press, 1997.

Harrison, Tony, *Selected Poems*, Penguin, 1984.

Havel, Vaclav, *Summer Meditations*, Knopf, 1992.

Hull, John M. *Touching the Rock: An Experience of Blindness*, Arrow Books, 1991.

Kamerman, J. B. *Death in the Midst of Life: Social and Cultural Influences on Death, Grief and Mourning*, Prentice Hall, 1988.

Kaufman, Shirley, "Intifada: The Status Quo," in *Rivers of Salt*, Copper Canyon Press, 1993.

Klass, Dennis, Silverman, Phyllis R., and Nickman, Steven, L.N., (eds.) *Continuing Bonds: New Understandings of Grief*, Taylor and Francis, 1996.

Lamm, Maurice, *The Jewish Way in Death and Mourning*, Jonathan David Publishers, 1969.

Lifton, Robert J., *Boundaries*, Random House, 1967.

Lipsett, Suzanne, *Surviving a Writer's Life*, HarperCollins, 1995.

Lopata, H., *Widowhood in an American City*, Schenckman, 1973.

McCarthy, Mary, *Memories of a Catholic Childhood*, Penguin, 1957.

Owen, Wilfred, *Collected Poems*, Chatto & Windus, 1963.

Parkes, Colin M. and Weiss, Robert S., *Recovery from Bereavement*, Basic Books, 1983.

Piaget, J., *The Language and Thought of the Child*, Routledge, and Kegan Paul, 1932.

Rutter, Michael and Marjorie, *Developing Minds*, Basic Books, 1992.

Shakespeare, William, *Collected Works*.

Silverman, Phyllis, R., *Widow to Widow*, Springer, 1986.

Sprang, Ginny and McNeil, John, *The Many Faces of Bereavement*, Brunner/Mazel, 1995.

Stroebe, M., Stroebe, W., and Hansson, R. (eds.), *Handbook of Bereavement*, Cambridge University Press, 1993.

Tanslea, Tangea, *For Women Who Grieve: Embracing Life After the Death of Your Partner*, Crossing Press, 1996.

Tisdall, E., *Queen Victoria's Private Life*, Jarrolds, 1952.

Visser, Margaret, *The Rituals of Dinner*, Penguin, 1992.

Wallace, William, *Living Again: A Personal Journey for Surviving the Loss of a Spouse*, Addax Publishing Group, 1998.

Walsh, Froma and McGoldrick, Monica, *Living Beyond Loss*, Norton, 1991.

Weenolsen, P. *Transcendence of Loss Over the Life Span*, Hemisphere, 1988.

Weiss, Robert S., *Loneliness*, MIT Press, 1973.

Weiss, Robert S., *Going It Alone*, Basic Books, 1979.

Weiss, Robert S., Loss and Recovery. *Journal of Social Issues*, Vol. 44, No. 3, pp. 37-52, 1988.

Wieseltier, Leon, *Kaddish*, Picador, 1998.

Zonnebelt-Smeenge, Susan J. and Devries, Robert, *Getting to the Other Side of Grief: Overcoming the Loss of a Spouse*, Baker Book House, 1999.